Down's Syndrome and the Family

the early years

Down's Syndrome and the Family

the early years

ANN GATH

Consultant Child Psychiatrist,
Borocourt Hospital, Wyfold, Reading, England

1978

 ACADEMIC PRESS

LONDON ● NEW YORK ● SAN FRANCISCO

A Subsidiary of Harcourt Brace Jovanovich Publishers

ACADEMIC PRESS INC. (LONDON) LTD.
24/28 Oval Road,
London NW1

United States Edition published by
ACADEMIC PRESS INC.
111 Fifth Avenue
New York, New York 10003

Library of Congress Catalog Card Number: 77–92819
ISBN: 0–12–277450–7

Text set in 11/12 pt Monotype Baskerville, printed by letterpress, and bound in Great Britain
by Robert MacLehose and Company Limited, Printers to the University of Glasgow

Acknowledgements

This research was funded by a grant from the Mental Health Research Fund which was kindly underwritten by the Variety Club of Great Britain. I am most grateful for the financial support and for the advice in planning the research given by the Steering Committee appointed by the fund consisting of Professor K. Rawnsley, Dr. Neil O'Connor and Professor G. W. Brown.

I am also grateful for the assistance of Mrs. Susan Peach and Mrs. Juliet Edmonds. Miss Tawnley, Miss Chris Fry and Miss Raine Huffam kindly undertook the typing.

Contents

Introduction

The Abnormal Baby

A baby that is less than perfect is always a shock to its parents (Drotar
et al., 1975). Large families and infant deaths were common one hundred
years ago; however, infant mortality has decreased (Butler and Alberman, 1969) and there has been a steady fall in the birth rate, particularly
since 1964 when the use of the contraceptive pill became widespread.
Expectations of the planned baby are great. There is increasing parental
awareness of their role in the birth process with more fathers present at
the delivery and more mothers wanting an active say in how they are to
be delivered. With all this planning and eager anticipation for the event,
the pain and disappointment of an abnormal baby is now intensified.
Grief following the birth of a malformed child has been described by
Solnit and Stark (1961) and the stages of mourning are further docu-
mented by the findings of Drotar *et al.* (1975).

The malformation may bring with it physical handicaps, mental
handicaps or a combination of both. Some defects are remediable. A
cleft lip has an exaggerated appearance in a newborn child and this can
greatly distress the parents (Slutsky, 1969). Offers of surgery with
encouraging photographs of similar children before and after operation,
however, bring hope and most parents are pleased with the result of
surgery (Gath, 1972). In contrast, operations on children with spina
bifida do not always alleviate the suffering of the child and the family
(Lorber, 1971) and the parents, as well as doctors, can find themselves
caught in an agonizing dilemma (de Lange, 1975).

The expectation of life may be normal or diminished and it is very
difficult to give parents any clear prognostic opinion. Parents of multi-
handicapped children in long stay hospitals commonly say that the child
was not expected to survive the first few months. Some of these parents
went through their grief at that time but years later are still confronted
by the fact that they have a severely malformed child.

The nature of the malformations, the medical and surgical interventions possible and the combination of the effects of handicap and of the demands of the treatment, if available, are all factors that determine the future life that can be envisaged for the child and the family.

Mental handicap is not remediable by surgery but its incidence and severity can be modified by high standards of antenatal care (Turnbull and Woodford, 1976), by modern neonatal care (Davies *et al.*, 1972), by environmental influences, particularly in the home (Centerwall and Centerwall, 1960) and by special education (Clarke and Clarke, 1974). Genetically determined conditions can never be "cured" and no amount of intervention will make the child normal. The diagnosis of such an abnormality does forecast a life of at least relative, and sometimes complete, dependency.

A baby with Down's syndrome has a characteristic appearance which, in most cases, is recognized by the nurses and doctors present at the birth, and may also be noticed by parents or other relatives. From the start their child's abnormality and all its implications confronts the parents. Very early in life such a child will look different from other children and the parents know that there is an almost certain prognosis of lasting mental handicap. This book examines the impact of this realization upon the parents and their other children during the first two years following the birth of a baby with Down's syndrome (mongolism).

Down's Syndrome (Mongolism)

Although cretinism has been referred to in medical writing since the time of Hippocrates, it was not until 1866 that Seguin described what was thought to be a variant of cretinism, which he referred to as the furfuraceous type. This paper of Seguin's was regarded by Penrose (1969) as the earliest clinical description of Down's syndrome which owes its name to Langdon Down who published his paper on the condition in 1866, when he referred to it as "mongolian idiocy" and postulated his theory of the ethnic causation of mental deficiency.

It is surprising that the affected children were not recognized and described before because their appearance makes them superficially alike and distinguishable from other people. One school of Spanish painters in the fifteenth century depicted the infant Christ as having features reminiscent of Down's syndrome. It is possible that their different looks and particularly their slanting eyes made babies with Down's syndrome the origin of the folklore about "changeling" children who were believed to have been placed in the cradle by the fairies when they stole the real baby.

Down's syndrome is now known to be due to a chromosomal abnormality. The affected children have slanting eyes due to palpebral tissues that are oblique and narrow towards the outside. Because of this and the presence of the epicanthic fold, there is a superficial resemblance to Orientals, which impressed Langdon Down.

However, children with Down's syndrome are found in all races. A typical Japanese child with the condition looks as different from other Japanese children as an affected European child does from normal Europeans (Matsunaga, 1967). The features are much closer together and there is usually flattening of the nose, a larger, fissured and often protruding tongue and frequently ear anomalies, of which an angular overlapping helix is the most common (Penrose, 1969). There is often mention in paediatric textbooks of Brushfield's spots which are light raised areas on the iris giving it a speckled appearance. Convergent squints occur in about a third of the affected children.

Children with Down's syndrome are usually short. Typically, their hands are broad, with short fingers, particularly a short curved fifth finger and a characteristic dermatoglyphic pattern (Scully, 1973). They often have particularly mobile joints in childhood which is due partly to lax ligaments and partly to hypotonia, or lack of muscle tone, which is most evident in the first year. The muscles develop more tone as the child grows, and in adults hypertonia is more common (Owens, 1971). A severe degree of hypotonia in infancy is likely to be associated with profound mental retardation (Penrose, 1972).

Associated congenital malformations are more frequently found in children with Down's syndrome. The most common associated abnormality is congenital heart disease which occurs in 30% of mongol children (Krovetz et al., 1969). An endocardial cushion defect, usually a complete atrioventricular canal, is the most common defect but ventricular septal defects and patent ductuses also commonly occur in conjunction with Down's syndrome, so that these three cardiac lesions make up 75% of the heart malformations associated with the condition.

Other congenital malformations which may be associated with Down's syndrome are gut anomalies such as oesophageal or duodenal atresia. These abnormalities give rise to major problems soon after birth and require surgical intervention to preserve the life of the child.

Mental handicap almost invariably accompanies Down's syndrome although isolated cases with intelligence quotients within the normal range have been reported. Most estimates of the mean I.Q. of groups of mongols are low. Penrose (1938) found a mean I.Q. of 22·8 in an institutionalized group, and later (Penrose, 1969) compared this figure with that found by Shipe and Shotwell (1964). Children brought up at home have a higher I.Q. than those in institutions (Centerwall and

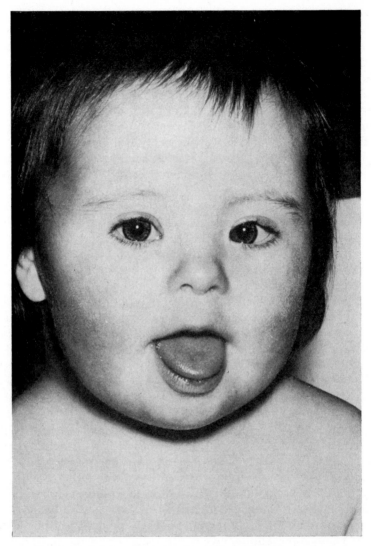

FIG. 1. Facial characteristics of a child with Down's syndrome.

Centerwall, 1960; Lyle, 1960a; Tizard, 1960). The findings of some researchers indicate that there is a decline in intelligence scores of children with Down's syndrome as they grow older. This decline cannot be explained by either social deprivation in the children or the verbal bias of the tests as children who had the stimulation of the constant company of normal young children were at least as likely to show this decline as those brought up by themselves (Carr, 1975) and the decline in D.Q. and I.Q. scores still occurred when verbal items were left out of the tests.

The term Down's syndrome is that most frequently used, in medical circles, to describe this condition, now known to be due to the presence of an extra chromosome 21. Other names in common usage are derived from Langdon Down's "mongolian idiot" and include "mongol" and "mongoloid defective". These names have been considered perjorative as well as inaccurate. Nonetheless, it was found that the majority of parents who have been interviewed in England by the author use the term "mongol" or "mongol child" and find it acceptable, more universally understood and less cumbersome than Down's syndrome. For this reason, the term "mongol" is used in this book.

1 Investigations into the Problems of Families with Handicapped Children

The Shift from Institutional Care

Since 1945, following the lead of Goldfarb (1945), Bowlby (1951) and Skodak and Skeels (1949), much attention has been paid to the harmful effects of bringing up children in an institution. If the environment of an institution can be shown to be detrimental to the cognitive and emotional development of children with no obvious organic pathology, it becomes difficult to argue that the same sort of institutional care can have positive advantages for children who are already showing delay in development due to congenital pathology.

In one comparative study of mongol and other retarded children reared at home and of similar children in an institution, the home reared children were found to walk earlier, to be better nourished and to have both intelligence and social quotients higher than those of the institution group (Centerwall and Centerwall, 1960). The home reared children were designated as moderately retarded or "trainable" in contrast to the institutional children who were severely retarded and "non-trainable". The children brought up in their own home for the first two-and-a-half years were thus shown to have considerable advantages over the children placed in institutions soon after birth, and these differences were apparent even after both groups had been in a state institution for some years.

Institutions obviously vary in quality and some are able to provide a more stimulating environment than others. Lyle (1959, 1960a) showed that institutionally reared children were particularly handicapped in language skills. Improvement of language was shown to occur when the children were placed in small groups which were "child centred" and which emphasized the formation of emotional relationships, as in the well-known Brooklands experiment (Lyle, 1960b; Tizard, 1960). Poor institutions produced additional handicaps, including effects on growth, but Stedman and Eichorn (1964) found that even the best institutional care they could provide, in an "enriched environment" in a special unit, still left their children, who were all mongols, lagging behind similar children reared at home in language and social skills. This particular study not only indicated the necessity of the individual care by parents but also the benefits to the retarded child of the company, stimulation, example and even competition of brothers and sisters.

Although, as Professor Jack Tizard pointed out in his Emmanuel Miller lecture in 1973, residential nurseries today are an improvement upon the institutions described in the classic studies of the forties and fifties, there is disturbing evidence, such as the description of the children's ward in the Ely report and from such books as "Put Away" by Pauline Morris and "The Empty Hours" by Maureen Osmin, to indicate that some institutions for the mentally retarded have not made the same degree of improvement.

There are therefore reasons to believe that most young mentally handicapped children do not benefit from institutional care. The concept of "community care" has developed and the accepted aim as put forward by Younghusband et al. (1970) is that the handicapped child should grow up in "a local community among ordinary people".

The Burden on the Family

Present planning of services focuses on the affected child and his family. Instead of a handicapped child being treated in isolation, there is now at least token consideration of the needs of a handicapped family consisting not only of parents and siblings but also of grandparents, uncles and aunts, who may exert a powerful influence on the more immediate or nuclear family. The key figures at the outset are the parents. It is they who are first told of their child's abnormality and it is they who must bear the responsibility for deciding the child's future. Moreover, the parents' attitudes are likely to play a major part in shaping the reactions of the brothers and sisters of the affected child.

In the well-known study by Tizard and Grad (1961) the "burden of care" upon the families of the handicapped children living at home is contrasted with the nearly normal lives of families of institutionalized children. But in this, as in the Australian group studies by Schonell and Watts (1957) and the Sheffield families described by Holt (1957) it has been difficult to separate the physical from the mental handicap. Many of the groups of children in these and other research are mixed, and the degree of physical capacity varies from total helplessness to robust health with abundant energy. Since physical handicap may mean that parents have to do heavy nursing in addition to their ordinary housework, it is not easy to assess what effect the fact of subnormality has upon the parents or rest of the family and what part of the stress can be attributed to the necessity of arduous physical work.

An additional complicating factor in interpreting the work of Holt (1957) and Schonell and Watts (1957) is that in both areas at that time training centres or other day care facilities were woefully inadequate and so the children concerned were often at home all day.

The majority of studies of the families with subnormal children suffer from two main disadvantages, their lack of proper control groups and the lack of objective data because of over-dependence on information from the mothers. Wolfensberger (1968) in his detailed review concludes:

> Until families of the retarded are carefully matched with other families, and the two groups compared, we shall not be certain what the qualitative and quantitative long-range effects of a retarded child are.

It is also necessary to distinguish between the effect of the emotional shock of the birth of an abnormal child and the stress of the practical problems of bringing up a handicapped child. There are indications from the work done in South Wales upon families of children with spina bifida that the observed effects in the families of the babies who died differ in several clear ways from those effects observed in the families of the survivors (Tew *et al.*, 1974).

Little attention has been paid to the problems of mentally handicapped children and their families from a developmental point of view. Changes that occur in the family as both the affected child and the siblings grow up have not been studied and there has been little discussion on this topic.

Two studies of physically handicapped children and their families take into account the changes that take place. Minde *et al.* (1972) described forty-one physically handicapped children and their families and they attempted to collect objective, developmental data. They included the community as a variable, and they placed their reliance on retrospective data but with less emphasis on the mother–child dyad. The process of adaptation by the family to the handicap was noted partilarly, and this too was the central theme of a prospective study of children with poliomyelitis by Davis (1963). Relationships within the family and particularly between the children were affected by the changes in the affected child.

As mongol children are handicapped from birth, or indeed from conception, their brothers and sisters will not have to readjust to marked changes. But as the affected child grows up his relationships with his brothers and sisters will change. Like all children, the mongol child changes from a helpless infant to a more active member of the family, but he will differ from other children in this rate of development and in his final level of achievement.

Planning of the Study

In this book particular attention is paid to siblings of the abnormal child. Parents, in the early days of the initial crisis of facing the fact of the handicap, say that although they themselves may feel obliged to take on responsibility for their own child, whether handicapped or not, they feel much more reluctant to accept responsibility on behalf of their other children. Parents of the mongol baby want to know if, by bringing up a handicapped child at home, they will jeopardize the future of their normal children.

An earlier study (Gath, 1972) compared the brothers and sisters of children who had operations to repair cleft palates and hare lips with brothers and sisters of children who were mongols. The study was of a small sample of twenty mongol families and twenty cleft palate families. One finding was that neither the school age siblings of children with treated cleft lip and/or cleft palate, nor the school age siblings of mongols, had any greater degree of behavioural disturbance than control children as measured by parental and teachers' reports. The second finding was that more than half the mongol group of families were experiencing moderate or severe problems of management, whilst only two of the cleft lip/cleft palate families were meeting moderate difficulties. These findings were difficult to reconcile.

It was then decided that two different methods of approach were needed in the study of families of handicapped children.

Survey of Siblings of Mongol Children

One approach was similar to that used in the earlier study referred to above. Larger numbers of siblings were involved so that the chances of finding any difference, should that difference exist, were improved. In contrast to the earlier study, the study was limited to that of siblings of mongol children. The main aim of this particular investigation was to determine whether the siblings of mongol children would show a greater degree of psychiatric disturbance than other children in the same school class.

Other aims of this study were to compile a large enough sample to allow intra-group comparisons and to provide a frame of reference for determining how far the families studied by the second approach were representative. The study was essentially a postal survey. Three research instruments were used, a questionnaire designed to obtain basic demographic data, and then two standardized behavioural scales, devised by Rutter, which were sent for completion to the parents and teachers of the children concerned (Gath, 1973, 1974).

The Present Study

The other approach entailed more detailed study of a small number of families. The problems of management of the handicapped child and the coping mechanisms adopted by the families need to be assessed in relation to possible effects in terms of impairment of mental and physical health. This intensive study which forms the subject matter of this book had to take into account changes in time and so had to be prospective, starting as soon as possible after the birth of the abnormal baby. At this stage the follow up was limited to approximately two years. The emphasis throughout has been on establishing a friendly relationship with the families and so all the interviews were conducted in the home with the minimum of formality. Whenever possible a tape recorder was used to enable the interviews to be more relaxed than when notes have to be taken and to allow more data to be recorded.

Methods Employed

The collection of data was mainly achieved through the use of a semi-structured interview. Six interviews spread over two years were used, except in the last five cases enrolled in each group when five interviews over a period of eighteen months took place. Where only five interviews occurred, the second and third interviews were taken together.

Incorporated in the first, fourth and sixth interviews were parts of the Family Investigation Interview devised and described by Rutter and Brown (1966). These parts dealt with the measurement of parental expectations, prohibitions and interaction with the children in the family and were used to collect base-line information in the first interview and repeated in the sixth and last interview.

For base-line investigation of the parent's health and personality, the Eysenck Personality Inventory was used and the Malaise Inventory, a shortened version of the Cornell Medical Index, which was compiled and used by Rutter et al. (1970). The E.P.I. has been standardized for self-administration. The Malaise Inventory was chosen as a useful instrument to measure subjective feelings of ill health or "the grumble factor" (Rutter et al., 1970).

At the end of the study, the General Health Questionnaire (Goldberg, 1972) was administered to all parents. The G.H.Q. was designed to elicit non-psychotic disturbance in the past month and was thus suitable for measuring mental health of the parents in a sample month at the end of the study.

For the brothers and sisters, Rutter B_2 rating scale (Rutter *et al.*, 1970) was used twice in the prospective study, at the beginning and at the end. The teachers were asked to complete this behavioural rating scale which was also used for the sibling survey. The A_2 scale for parents, also used in the sibling survey, was employed only at the start when parents were asked to complete it at the first interview. At the end of the study, the ground was covered in the sixth interview when parents were asked about the siblings' health and behaviour, thus making the A_2 scale at this stage superfluous.

Younger siblings aged three and four years at the end of the study were investigated by means of Richman and Graham's (1971) behavioural rating scale for three-year-old children.

The mothers in the families were seen at every interview with one exception when the mother concerned was in hospital. Fathers were present at some interviews. Some fathers were present for most interviews but others for only one. All fathers in both groups were seen on at least one occasion. Younger children in the family were likely to be seen at least once. Where there were older children who were away at work and only home for occasional week-ends, these were not included in the study of the family.

2 The Families in the Prospective Study

Much of the information about families with handicapped children has come from sources that are unavoidably biased in one direction or another. A major source of this bias is referral artefact. Paediatricians are more likely to be asked to see those children who have medical problems in addition to delayed development due to intellectual impairment. In the paediatric wards, the mongol children who also have congenital heart disease are more frequently met and these patients will also have more intensive follow up care in out-patients than those mongol children who have features of the classic Down's syndrome but have no associated congenital malformation in addition. It is clear that those children who attract most of the paediatric attention are the more severely afflicted children with the double handicap of mongolism and congenital heart disease or gastro-intestinal anomaly. Such children may not survive the first two years and may never go to school or meet a teacher. In contrast, the teacher in special education will have more experience of the more physically healthy and it may well be the most robust children who imprint themselves most firmly upon the teacher's memory. There will be more overlap between teacher and psychiatrist as a psychiatric opinion is usually requested when a child develops a behavioural disorder at home or school. The psychiatrist's experience is, however, subject to another bias as his clinical practice in the hospitals will also include more of the very severely subnormal mongols than those whose intelligence more nearly approximates to the average range. Community social workers encounter mongol children incidentally as members of families who are trying to cope with the stresses of poverty, homelessness and breakdown of marriage as well as the stress of a mentally handicapped child. On the other hand, social workers have less opportunity of meeting the mongol child who is an accepted member of a happy and stable family.

The experience of the parents of a mentally handicapped child differs yet again from each of the professional groups. Some parents have written books or articles in the newspapers telling of their feelings when confronted with the crisis of producing a child with the congenital mental disability. These accounts are both moving and informative. They offer a new dimension to the knowledge acquired by the doctors, teachers, nurses and social workers. Much of the value in the parents' contributions to the literature of mental and physical handicap lies in the inevitably subjective and personal nature of the books and articles from those whose lives are most intimately affected by the problems. The experiences are very varied. The degree of handicap described varies from severe with associated poor physical health to an unusual degree of intelligence in a mongol (Hunt, 1967). Some parents who write about their mongol child have managed to bring him or her up throughout childhood in their own homes (Wilks and Wilks, 1974; Hunt, 1967) but in most of the other books or articles, particularly those published less recently, the parents tell of the problems that led them to seek long term care for the child away from home (Buck, 1951; Ashley Miller, 1971; Green, 1966). The experience of having a mentally handicapped child prompts other parents with different attributes to take an active part in societies or campaigns for similarly handicapped children and adults. The experiences and reactions of articulate parents, be they authors or action committee members, are well publicized but most of these parents are "middle class" and hardly representative of the majority of parents of mongol children.

Aims of the Study

The aim of the present study is to follow a group of families from as soon as possible after the birth of a mongol baby for a period of approximately two years. Thirty families only could be studied in depth. In order to draw any useful conclusions, it is necessary for this group of thirty to be a sample with the minimum of bias.

Identification of the Sample

All babies diagnosed as having Down's syndrome by a paediatrician and born in what was the area of the Oxford Regional Hospital Board on, or after, 1st January 1970 were eligible for inclusion in the sample to be studied, provided that they fulfilled the only criterion of being brought up within the family. The last baby to be enrolled, bringing up the numbers in the sample to thirty, was born in November 1971.

During the period in which the sample was being collected, forty babies known to be mongols were born in the area of the Oxford Regional Hospital Board. Ten were not enrolled in the study. Four babies died before they could be included. Two of these babies died of congenital heart disease, one of congenital leukaemia and the fourth had duodenal atresia and multiple congenital defects. The other children did not fulfil the criterion of living at home as part of the family. Three of these had been taken into the care of the local authority. One of the three in care was the illegitimate child of a seventeen-year-old girl but the other two were born to married women. Only one mongol baby was admitted to a subnormality hospital during the period January 1st 1970 to 30th November 1971. The tenth child enrolled in the study was a baby born to a private patient. No details were made available concerning this baby or its parents.

Only two of the thirty babies eventually forming the sample were born at home. The rest were born in hospital. Nine were born in the teaching hospital maternity unit, sixteen in the various district hospital maternity units and three in general practitioner maternity units. The hospitals were widely spread over the region, which extends from Corby in the north to Swindon in the south-west and High Wycombe and Reading in the east and south-east.

The main source of notifications of births of babies with known mongolism was through the Department of Population Genetics Research. Although all the paediatricians in the area had been informed of the study in advance, few notifications came direct from them.

Age at notification varied greatly. Some babies were only two weeks old when notified but others were much older including one who was already a year old when he was finally seen. Efforts were made to enrol all eligible babies despite the delays in notification. The late notified cases were often those about whom the paediatricians and general practitioners were most anxious. The doctors in charge of those cases had been reluctant to notify the cases early because they feared that a research worker entering what was judged to be a very delicate situation might precipitate some disturbance.

After notification of the cases eligible for the research, the general practitioners were contacted and asked if they would be agreeable to their patients participating in this research. They all agreed, but two family doctors asked for the first interview to be postponed for a short period until they felt the parents would be able to cope with a visit from a research worker. When the agreement of the general practitioner had been obtained, the parents were approached and asked if the investigator might visit them to explain the research and to enrol them in the study if possible.

No family in the group with a mongol baby refused to allow the investigator to visit them for the first interview. In one case, the mother asked if the interview could take place in the evening so that her husband could be present. This couple, whose mongol baby was their sixth child, were courteous and most hospitable. They took part in the first interview but then politely withdrew. They explained that they had conscientious objections to the use of questionnaires and to most other methods of data collection. They had also refused to complete the census form and, at the time of the interview, were waiting to see if legal steps could be taken against them.

Selection of the Control Group

The arrival of any baby, however healthy or welcome, affects the family into which it is born. The main aim of this study is to see if the birth of a mongol baby produces changes that are different in kind or degree from those changes encountered in families with normal babies. The families of the mongol babies were therefore carefully matched with control families with normal babies. The selection of the control families was accomplished in the following way. First, the index case, a family with a mongol child, was identified and the first visit to that family made. This initial interview provided the basic demographic data. At the time of the visit, the characteristics of the home environment was noted, including type of housing and the general features of the neighbourhood.

The control families were found through the maternity unit records of the teaching hospitals. It was possible through the kind co-operation of the obstetricians and midwives concerned to identify likely control families from the admission records and day books. A baby was selected who was born on the same day as the mongol baby or as near as possible to that date and who was of the same sex and ordinal position in family. From the records available in the maternity units, it was found possible to match father's occupation as being in the same socio-economic group and to find in most cases mothers whose ages approximated to that of the mothers of the index babies. Familiarity with the area served by the maternity units enabled the main characteristics of the home neighbourhood of the control baby to be comparable with those of the neighbourhood in which the mongol baby was being brought up.

A letter was sent to each possible control family asking permission to visit. Three families who were originally selected as possible controls could not be traced as they had moved away from the area since the birth of their baby. These three were replaced by the next possible case. One family considered as a possible control was visited but it was found that the description in the hospital records of the socio-economic status of the family was misleading and so the matching would have not been adequate. In one family, the husband telephoned immediately after getting the letter of introduction to say that he did not wish his family to take part and, in another family, the wife was happy to cooperate but her husband disagreed. Replacements were therefore found for these refusals. In all the other "normal" families who were approached and asked if they would help with the work there was a high degree of cooperation from both husbands and wives which continued throughout the period of study.

Finally over the period of two years thirty families with a young mongol child were enrolled in the study as index subjects and they were matched with thirty families of similar background and structure who had a normal child of the same sex and age.

Although the method of identification of families for this study was designed to eliminate as much selection bias as possible, it is still necessary to determine how representative was the final sample obtained. Two frames of reference were available for comparison with the sample. The first of these was the sibling study carried out in the same geographical area. Basic demographic data had been obtained during the course of this study of one hundred and four families with a mongol child and one or more other children of school age (Gath, 1973, 1974). The second frame of reference was the data obtained from the 1958 Perinatal Mortality Survey (Butler and Alberman, 1969) in which some information about the mongol children born in the sample week in March 1958 can be found.

Maternal Age

Non-dysjunction during meiosis in the development of the ovum is the cause of mongolism in 97% of cases, as explained in Chapter 8 of this book, and is associated with increasing maternal age. Although efforts were made in matching to approximate the age of the mother of the control baby to that of the mother of the mongol baby, the mothers of the mongols were older than those of the control children. The mean age of the mothers of the mongol babies was 31·63 years (standard deviation 8·02) and that of the mothers of the controls was 27·83 (standard deviation 5·77). However, the mothers in this sample of thirty mongol babies were slightly younger than those in the one hundred and four families in the sibling survey (mean age 33·39 years, standard deviation 6·36) and than the mothers of the mongols in the 1958 Perinatal Mortality Survey (mean age 34·2 years). Details of the distribution of the ages of the mothers in the populations compared are shown in Table 1.

Although Penrose (1961) showed that it was maternal age and not paternal age that is associated with a higher incidence of mongol births,

Table 1

Maternal age-percentages in each age group: prospective study groups and survey populations compared

Age group	Prospective study				Survey populations			
	Mongol group		Control group		Sibling survey		1958 Control week[a]	
	No.	%	No.	%	No.	%	No.	%
Under 20	0	0	1	3	0	0	978	6
20–24	9	30	6	20	12	12 ⎫	10,380	61
25–29	4	13	13	44	18	17 ⎭		
30–34	6	20	7	23	26	17	3422	20
35–39	3	10	0	0	26	25 ⎫	2203	13
40 +	8	27	3	10	20	19 ⎭		
TOTAL	30	100	30	100	104	100	16,994	100

[a] Perinatal Mortality Survey Control Week Population taking Singleton births only (Butler and Alberman, 1969)

the ages of fathers are closely correlated with that of the mothers. Once more fathers of the mongol babies in this prospective study were older than fathers of control babies with a mean age of 33·9 years (standard deviation 8·05) as compared with a mean age of 30·5 years (standard deviation 5·86). Fathers of the mongol babies in the group were, as were the mothers, slightly younger than the fathers in the sibling survey (mean age 35·5 years, standard deviation 7·38) and than the fathers of mongols in the 1958 survey (mean age 36·6 years).

Ordinal Position

Eleven of the mongol babies in the prospective study sample were first born children. Seven of the mongols were second children, ten were third children and one was the fourth child in the family. For each of these babies, a control child was found who had the same position in the

Table 2

Ordinal position of mongol children

Ordinal position	Prospective study sample		Sibling study sample	
	No.	%	No.	%
First born	11	37	13	12
Second born	7	23	42	41
Third born	10	33	18	17
Fourth or subsequent	2	7	31	30
TOTAL	30	100	104	100

birth order. One mongol was the tenth child and was the only baby born in the area of the main teaching hospital to a mother who had had more than five previous children. The best match for him was a sixth child.

There were relatively more first born children in the prospective study sample than in the sibling survey group of mongols. Thirty-seven per cent of the babies in the smaller group were first born children, as compared with 12% of the mongols from the sibling study sample. There were also less fourth and subsequent born mongol children in the prospective study than had been found in the sibling study (Table 2). So in this group of thirty, there were probably too many small families and too few large families to be truly representative of the families with mongol children in the area as a whole.

Social Class of the Families

The Registrar General's classification of occupations was used to determine the social class of the family by the job of the father. Five families were in social class I, nine in social class II, eleven in social class III, two in social class IV and three in social class V. The distribution by social class was very similar to that found in the sibling survey sample of families except that social class IV, semi-skilled workers, were less frequently found in the prospective sample. Since father's occupation was one of the criteria used in matching, there was no social class difference between the mongol families and the control families in the study.

The level of education achieved by the parents is naturally closely associated with father's occupation. No information about the educational standards achieved by the parents in the sibling study was available for comparison with the parents in the prospective sample. Since, as has been said, the families were matched for father's occupational status, there were no appreciable differences between the mongol fathers and the control fathers in the amount of further training they had received after school and only very small differences in the educational achievements. The mothers of the normal control babies were however slightly less likely to have stayed on at school to take O and A levels than were the mothers of the mongol babies.

Area and Neighbourhood

The families for the sibling survey were collected from the same geographical area as were the families in the prospective study. The area, that of the then Oxford Regional Board, consisted of the whole or part of five counties and of three county boroughs making a total of eight local authorities. Provisions for mentally handicapped children were known to vary considerably from one local authority to another within the general area of what was the Regional Hospital Board. The geographical distribution of the families according to which local authority area they were living was very similar in the prospective study sample and in the sibling survey sample. Areas with exceptionally good facilities for the mentally handicapped were as well represented as those areas with less community provision. Similarly the sample of thirty families included some from the commuter areas of the south and east, some from the industrial new towns in the north and some from the more rural areas more often found in the west of the region.

Homes of the Families

Eighteen (60%) of the houses of the mongol group of families were owner-occupied, very slightly more than in the control group. The rest of the homes of the mongol families were either council houses or privately rented houses. Two of the control families who were of the same standing as most of the owner occupiers, had houses provided by their employers. No data was available on the proportion of owner–occupiers amongst the sibling survey families.

There were slightly more control families who lived in rural areas than there were families of mongol babies. The immediate neighbourhoods of each pair were, however, as similar as possible. The large estates in the rapidly growing villages could still be described as rural but had much in common with suburban estates particularly with regard to atmosphere and amenities.

At the start of the study more of the parents of the mongol babies were happily settled in their homes as twenty-four (80%) expressed satisfaction. Slightly less control families (eighteen or 60%) were as pleased with their homes. The dissatisfied families in the mongol group included two couples living in furnished accommodation and one family in an unfurnished flat which was damp and very expensive to heat. Two control couples were living with the maternal grandparents. One control couple officially owned their house but this was in name only as the paternal grandparents were in possession, allowing the young couple and their three children only one room to call their own. All three couples living with "in-laws" expressed dissatisfaction with their home conditions at the outset of the study but more council tenants and owner–occupiers in the control group wanted to move than did families of mongols in similar circumstances.

One family in each group had only an outside toilet. The three control families mentioned previously had to share a bathroom with the grandparents. There were no significant differences between the two groups of families in the possession of other amenities or luxuries such as possession of washing machines, cars, television sets or telephones in the home.

The families with a mongol baby had lived in their present home for a mean of four years (standard deviation 4·25) and the control families had spent a mean of 2·8 years (standard deviation 2·39) in the house in which they were living. There was no evidence that the control group had more or less stable homes than the mongol group, since there was no significant difference in the number of homes the families in each group had had since marriage nor in the number of jobs that the father in the family had had in the past five years.

Social Contacts

Since the families into which a mongol baby is born can only be identified after the event, much of the base-line data is retrospective and liable to bias. In order to keep this bias to a minimum. the families were asked factual questions covering a specific period of time. Family functioning up to the time of the latest, index, birth was measured by dating the number of holidays in the past three years and by rating the social outlets in the year immediately before the birth.

Half the mongol families and nearly half the control families had had an annual holiday in each of the three years before the index birth. But as can be seen in Table 3, more than twice as many mongol families had had no holiday in the past three years.

In their social activities, the control families were more likely to have close contact with maternal grandparents ($X^2 = 5·32$, d.f. $= 1$, p $<0·05$). There was a similar but less marked difference in the contact with the paternal grandparents and with the brothers and sisters of the fathers. The parents of the control babies also had tended to go out together more frequently than did the parents of the mongol babies, but in this, the difference just failed to reach a significant level.

The small sample of thirty families with a new born mongol baby has been shown to be, on the whole, a representative sample of families with

Table 3

Family holidays in the three years before the index birth

	Mongol family	Control family
Holiday every year	15	14
Holiday once or twice	6	12
No holiday in past three years	9	4
	30	30

mongol children in the area. The matching procedure to select the control families had produced a group with similar social and economic characteristics and the more detailed information available at the first interview indicates that the matching on these points was good. Yet there are differences in the ways the families functioned up to the point in time when the baby, the focal point of this study, was born. These differences will be taken into account when changes occurring during the period of study are assessed.

3 The Two Groups of Babies

Prenatal Influences on Mothers and Babies

The psychological development of the child is influenced by inter-action of environmental factors with genetic factors. A continuous series of effects and counter effects starts from conception. Folk-lore contains many warnings about possible damage that may occur to the unborn child if the mother has a frightening experience or encounters an unusual event. Although many of these "old wives tales" are regarded as mere superstition, the uterus is not thought of as a completely safe haven and more attention is being paid to the hazards of intra-uterine life.

It has been clear at least for thirty years that physical illness in the mother during pregnancy can have adverse effects upon the foetus. Some maternal diseases directly affect the supply of oxygen or nutrients to the developing foetus as in toxaemia of pregnancy and in diabetes, whilst illnesses produced by certain pathogens, particularly viruses, may infect the foetus itself as in rubella, toxoplasmosis or syphilis. Much more recently, it has become apparent that social and psychological stresses experienced by a mother during her pregnancy may also have an ad-verse effect on the delivery or on the early development of the infant.

In a recent review of the research in this area (Sameroff and Chandler, 1974) it has been shown that much of the data has been gathered retro-spectively and that many studies have other methodological drawbacks, such as lack of proper controls. Nevertheless, it is apparent that anxiety and other disruptive emotional experiences in pregnancy are associated with a high degree of complications of pregnancy, delivery and infant morbidity.

Emotional stress in pregnancy has been specifically associated with the birth of an abnormal child. Stott (1961) and Drillien and Wilkinson (1964) both found that mothers of mongol children reported more emotional shocks in the first three months of pregnancy than did the mothers of other mentally handicapped children, who were incapaci-tated to the same degree as were the mongol children. An explanation given for these findings is that the emotional stress, which cannot be cited as the cause of the chromosomal abnormality, acts by inhibiting what would be the natural abortion of malformed foetuses (Stott, 1969). Further work by Drillien and Wilkinson (1964a) with mothers of children with cleft palate/cleft lip did not produce convincing evidence that mothers of such children had had more emotional trauma than had mothers of normal children. Dissatisfaction is expressed by these workers with the definition of emotional distress and its measurement, particularly by questionnaire administered retrospectively.

Stott (1973) has found that social and emotional problems in pregnancy, including marital discord, are significantly associated with ill-health, neurological dysfunction, developmental slowing and disturbances of behaviour in the baby. There is some indication from this study that it is the tension engendered in the mother who cannot cope with her environment that is particularly associated with increased morbidity in the infant. Social factors such as poverty or overcrowding, and psychological factors such as marital discord between the parents, have an effect on child rearing that has been shown to outweigh and outlast perinatal stress as a cause of disability in childhood (Werner *et al.*, 1971; Davie *et al.*, 1972; Wedge and Prosser, 1973).

Characteristics of the baby itself influence the parent/child relationship (Korner, 1973). The studies of Thomas *et al.* (1968) suggest that the temperament of the baby may influence parental behaviour, producing an effect lasting long into childhood. These temperamental differences can be observed in very young babies (Carey, 1970) and are noticeable particularly in the level of activity in irritability and in regularity of sleeping and feeding. These differences may be factors determining how easy or difficult a child is to bring up (Rutter *et al.*, 1975). Irritability and, in particular, constant crying do have an effect on parental behaviour. Studies of battered babies have indicated that an immature parent may feel rejected by the persistent crying of a baby (Kempe and Helfer, 1972) and, particularly in adverse social circumstances, may damage the child. Other parents are more irritated by a passive and unresponsive baby.

The situation becomes yet more complex as pregnancy complications or foetal abnormality due to genetic causes may lead to admission to a special care neonatal nursery where the baby will be separated from the mother and nursed in a sometimes noisy environment with procedures that may be stressful to the baby itself and to the parents when they visit. The effect of separation from the mother and baby as well as the anxiety arising from the baby's condition may lead not only to long standing effects on the relationship between mother and child (Kennell and

Klaus, 1974) but also to disturbances in the relationship between the parents (Liederman, 1974).

Although mongolism is a chromosomal abnormality determined during the development of the ovum before even conception occurs, the experiences of pregnancy may still exert an influence on the child and its parents and may also affect the early development and social interactions of the apparently healthy control child.

The Planning of the Pregnancies in the Two Groups

Although the majority of the mothers of both the mongol babies and the normal controls had welcomed the latest pregnancy which had ended in the birth of the index baby in this study, eleven of the mothers of mongols and ten of the mothers of controls said that the pregnancy had been unplanned, accidental or "had come as a bit of a surprise". Thus in each group, one third of the pregnancies had been unplanned, a similar finding to that of Cartwright (1970) in her study of parents and family planning. In Vesey's survey (1975) of women attending family planning clinics, the proportion of "planned" births was 78·3%, "unplanned, unwanted" births 16·7% and "unplanned, wanted" births 5%. In Vesey's sample, all the mothers had been recruited for the survey through a family planning clinic. In the population as a whole, the proportion of planned births falls with a corresponding rise in the proportion of unplanned but not necessarily unwanted births, because of the reluctance of a significant proportion of women to use family planning clinics and to rely instead on such methods of contraception as the sheath, withdrawal or the rhythm or "safe period" method.

Significantly more of the mothers of thirty-five or more in the mongol group had conceived accidentally (Table 4). There is also an excess of unplanned pregnancies in the youngest group of mothers of mongols who were less than twenty-five at the birth. The control group also shows a peak of unplanned pregnancies in the mothers who were less than twenty-five when the index baby was born. The numbers of mothers in both groups who had an accidental pregnancy in their early twenties reflects the pattern of the population as a whole.

The five women under thirty-five who had given birth to a mongol after an unplanned pregnancy had all intended to have another child at some time but they had conceived earlier than had been intended. None of these women were distressed by the pregnancy and the babies were definitely "wanted" by the time the pregnancy had entered the third trimester. Three of these mothers had already had one or two children and the other two had become pregnant very soon after marriage. No mongol baby was born within nine months of the parents' marriage.

Table 4

Planned and unplanned pregnancies in the
mongol group

Age range	Planned	Unplanned	TOTAL
35 and over	4	7	11
34 and under	14	5	19
TOTAL	18	12	30

$X^2 = 10 \cdot 3$, d.f. $= 1$, p $< 0 \cdot 01$

Three control babies had been conceived premaritally. although none of the three marriages can be described as forced by the pregnancy as all three pairs had definite intentions to get married. The pregnancy may have been inconvenient but was in no case a disaster and the mothers were not distressed by the hurried wedding.

Only one of the seven mothers over the age of thirty-five who gave birth to a mongol after an accidental pregnancy was a primigravida. This particular woman had been married for fourteen years. She had not wanted children although her husband would have dearly loved to have a child. She was distressed when she first realized that she was pregnant, but quickly became reconciled to the idea and had finally come to look forward eagerly to the child.

Four mothers, having third or fourth children, were able to accept the last unplanned pregnancy easily. Another woman who had a third pregnancy twelve years after her last child was initially very upset, but by the time her child was due to be born, both she and her husband were pleased at the prospect of a new baby and had enjoyed making plans, choosing a pram and collecting a layette.

Severe emotional distress can be said to have occurred in only one of the seven unplanned pregnancies in older women and in none of the unplanned pregnancies to younger women. The wife in this exception was over forty and had two daughters who were aged eleven and eight when the mongol boy was born. The husband knew about the increased risk of mongolism in older women and he was also worried about his wife's history of hypertension. They decided to ask for an abortion when the pregnancy was confirmed by the family doctor and requested a referral to a gynaecologist. When the wife was seen there was some confusion over her dates and the couple were told that the pregnancy was too far advanced for an abortion to be carried out safely. The father was very bitter about the decision, particularly as the mother had to spend nearly eight weeks in hospital before the birth of the child. In con-

B

trast, the mother, although greatly distressed by the upheaval, was much less resentful of the coming child.

Severe emotional distress also occurred in a pregnancy that was originally planned. The wife, who was thirty-five at the birth, had stopped taking oral contraceptives one year before conception and she had very much wanted to become pregnant. The relationship between this woman and her husband then deteriorated to the point that the couple agreed to separate before it was realized that the wife was indeed pregnant. Their first reaction was to seek a referral to a private abortion clinic and then to proceed with their plans for a separation. Although the husband had had two sons by a previous marriage, the wife had never been pregnant before and she began to appreciate that she was unlikely to have another chance of a child. She found that she was unable to go through with her plans for an abortion and so she and her husband resolved to mend their marriage for the sake of the coming child. Unfortunately, the marriage finally broke down when the father could not accept the baby after he had been told that the child was a mongol six weeks after birth.

Length of Pregnancy and Birth Weight

The mongol babies were more frequently born before the end of the thirty-eighth week of gestation. Eleven mongols and only three controls were more than two weeks early by their mothers' estimates of the dates of their last normal periods.

Eleven mongol babies (37%) were less than six pounds at birth whilst all the control babies weighed more than this. These mongols were nearly all "small for dates", weighing less than the expected weight for gestational age. Penrose and Smith (1966) quotes the findings of Smith and McKeowen (1955) who reported 52% of their series of mongols had birth weights below six pounds, but the group who make up the subjects of the present study do not include those mongols who died too early to be enrolled.

Special Care in the Neonatal Period

There is a marked difference between the mongol group and the control group in the numbers of babies who were nursed in special care baby units. Twenty-five (83%) of the mongols were in special care nurseries for at least two days as compared with only four (13%) of the control babies. Six of the mongols were kept in the special care units for more than one month but no control baby stayed in hospital for longer than ten days. The six who were in hospital for a long period were undoubtedly in a precarious state of health for a large proportion of the first month of life, while others in the units for shorter periods were initially difficult to feed and required tube feeding. Yet, from the accounts given by the mothers, some who had spent several days in the special care baby units had had no particular problems, medical or management, and may perhaps have been kept away from their mothers solely because the diagnosis of mongolism was known or suspected.

Breast or Bottle Feeding

Despite the fact that so many more of the mongol babies were separated from their mothers in the neonatal period, the number of mongols who were breast fed was very similar to the number of breast fed normal babies. Eight of the mongols (27%) and seven (23%) of the control babies were breast fed for at least one month.

Difficulties in feeding are frequently found in mongols who have a severe associated anomaly (Penrose, 1970). Two of the babies with congenital heart disease were very difficult to feed because of dyspnoea and cyanotic attacks. Feeding these two infants was a harrowing experience for the mothers and each feed during the first three months took an average of one-and-a-half hours to complete. Six of the other mongols were very slow suckers or "lazy feeders" and so were two of the control babies. Feeding these eight babies was time consuming and some of the mothers found it difficult to be patient, particularly when there were other small children about. None of the control babies presented problems in feeding that were as difficult as the two mongols who had severe heart disease but two normal babies had what appeared to be moderately severe problems in feeding. One of these babies, a boy who was a second child, vomited profusely after nearly every feed until he was eight months old. His mother was concerned but was reassured by her general practitioner that nothing was wrong. The baby, however, looked thin and miserable and gained weight only very slowly. He began to thrive when the vomiting stopped at eight months, after which he was a contented, easy to manage child. This child's symptoms were more severe than those of the other control child who had moderately severe feeding problems but the mother of the second was much more anxious and, as a result, the feeding difficulties of her child, despite adequate weight gain, were more disruptive of the household organization than were any of the difficulties presented by the mongol babies in the first year.

As Penrose says, many of the mongols were "good" and made little demands on their mother's attention. This tendency to sleep peacefully between feeds and to show reduced responses to hunger or discomfort was particularly evident in the behaviour at night. Twenty-three mongol babies (77%) did not wake their mother for a night feed regularly after the first two weeks at home, but only nine (30%) of the control babies slept through the night at that stage.

Appearance of the Babies

All the mongols had the characteristic Down's syndrome features in that they had epicanthic folds, eyes that appeared to be slanted, features bunched together in the centre of the face, a flattened profile and a flattened occiput. These features were much more obvious in some children than in others. Some babies could be recognized very easily as mongols by a quick glance. Two babies (referred to by the codes M5 and M17 in Table 5) had much less pronounced Down's syndrome features and were quite frequently not recognized as "mongols", even by the general practitioner in one case. The two babies who were known to be mosaics, with some cells containing 47 chromosomes and others with the normal 46, were not distinguishable by their appearance from the other babies in this group and were both in fact more "typical mongols" than either of the two previously referred to in whom no evidence of mosaicism was found by chromosome examination at the Population Genetics Research Unit in Oxford.

Physical Abnormalities

The physical abnormalities found in the two groups of babies are listed in Table 5. The two most common findings in the mongols were signs of congenital heart disease and abnormalities of muscle tone.

Fourteen (47%) of the mongols had signs of congenital heart lesions. This incidence is slightly less than the incidence of cardiac anomalies obtained from post-mortem studies and very similar to the incidence found in clinical or out-patient samples, as reviewed by Penrose (1969). Eight mongols had systolic murmurs but no other symptoms. Three further children had no symptoms or impairment of growth or activity but had systolic murmurs accompanied by an easily palpable thrill. Three of the mongols were seriously incapacitated by the congenital heart lesion and were cyanotic and dyspnoeic, particularly during feeds or after even mild activity. One of these three babies had gross cyanosis all the time and he also had clubbing of the fingers. He was known to have Fallot's Tetralogy, found in 1% of mongols with congenital heart disease, according to Rowe and Uchida's series quoted by Penrose (1969).

The abnormality of muscle tone, commonly found in this group of mongols, was a reduction in tone, particularly of the muscles of the back, neck and limbs. Only five (16%) of the mongol children examined at the second interview had normal muscle tone. Six (20%) had mild hypo-

Table 5

Physical abnormalities of index babies—mongols

Code	Sex	Signs of congenital heart disease	Muscle tone	Other abnormalities
1	F	systolic murmur only	normal	squint
2	M	systolic murmur only	moderate hypotonia	—
3	F	—	moderate hypotonia	umbilical hernia
4	F	—	mild hypotonia	—
5	M	—	normal	—
6	F	systolic murmur, cyanosis, enlarged liver	severe hypotonia	—
7	F	systolic murmur	mild hypotonia	umbilical hernia
8	M	—	moderate hypotonia	—
9	M	—	moderate hypotonia	—
10	F	—	moderate hypotonia	pallor, renal tract abnormality
11	F	systolic murmur, cyanosis, enlarged liver	severe hypotonia	pallor
12	M	—	severe hypotonia	umbilical hernia, failure to thrive, unresponsive
13	M	systolic murmur	moderate hypotonia	—
15	M	—	normal	—
16	F	systolic murmur	mild hypotonia	—
17	M	—	normal	—
18	M	—	mild hypotonia	—
19	F	—	moderate hypotonia	—
20	M	—	severe hypotonia	—
21	M	systolic murmur and thrill	mild hypotonia	—
22	M	—	normal	—
23	M	systolic murmur	mild hypotonia	—
24	M	—	moderate hypotonia	bilateral cataract
25	F	systolic murmur	moderate hypotonia	squint
26	M	systolic murmur, large heart cyanosis, dyspnoeic clubbing	moderate hypotonia	—
27	M	—	moderate hypotonia	—
28	M	systolic murmur and thrill	severe hypotonia	—
29	F	—	moderate hypotonia	—
30	M	systolic murmur and thrill	moderate hypotonia	—
31	F	systolic murmur	inert, ill, severe hypotonia	—

Control babies:

Only abnormalities were:

Code	Sex	Signs of congenital heart disease	Muscle tone	Other abnormalities
C8	M	—	—	thin, hungry baby
10	F	—	—	eczema on face and neck
15	M	—	—	strawberry naevus on head
23	M	—	—	strawberry naevus on chest

tonia, thirteen (43%) had moderate hypotonia and six (20%) had severe hypotonia. Cowie (1970) related the degree of hypotonia to gestational age in her study of the neurological development of mongols. In the term related age range of two to thirteen weeks, she found 27% to be extremely hypotonic, 45% markedly hypotonic and 3% moderately hypotonic, with none with normal tone. At sixteen to thirty weeks of term-related age, Cowie found 6% to be extremely hypotonic, 36% markedly hypotonic and 58% moderately hypotonic. In the present series, most of the mongols were, at the time of the second interview, aged in the second age group quoted by Cowie, and it was found too that the degree of hypotonia decreased with age. Only one baby remained severely hypotonic throughout the period of study.

No control baby was found to have a serious congenital defect. All had normal heart sounds with no murmurs. All had normal muscle tone. Two of the control baby boys had strawberry naevi, neither of which was seriously disfiguring and both faded away before completion of the study. One girl had mild eczema of her face and neck when examined at the second interview and this persisted through the first year, improving in the second. The boy who had persistent vomiting after feeds was a thin irritable baby when seen at the second interview. As mentioned above, he improved rapidly after eight months and, in his second year, was an attractive, healthy little boy.

Deaths During the Period of Study

Five deaths occurred during the period of study in the mongol group. Four of the deaths were to children with congenital heart disease. One of the babies who became cyanotic and dyspnoeic on feeding died at the age of seven months and the boy with Fallot's Tetralogy died at the age of two years four months. Two other children who had had systolic murmurs died of bronchopneumonia in the first year. One baby who had severe symptoms of congenital heart disease improved in her second year and was continuing to gain weight with diminution of symptoms when the period of study came to an end.

The fifth death in the series was that of a boy who was one of the two with minimal signs of mongolism. He had been very healthy, had no signs or symptoms of congenital heart disease and had developed physically and mentally within normal limits. He became ill at the age of two years and died three weeks after the onset of acute lymphatic leukaemia.

Not surprisingly, more of the mongol babies were admitted to hospital after the neonatal period than were the controls. Two of the deaths, however, occurred to children who had had no in-patient treatment before they died. In both these cases, there was some lack of communication between the mother and her general practitioner who was thought by the parents to have not appreciated the severity of the child's symptoms. One of these babies was the boy with Fallot's Tetralogy. He had been well in the neonatal period but had had attacks in which he appeared to be in pain. These early attacks were thought to be due to "three month colic" by the family doctor or so he told the mother. Later on unmistakeable signs of severe dyspnoea, cyanosis and clubbing appeared. The baby was treated as an out-patient but his attacks became worse despite medication and he finally died.

The mother's accounts of what the general practitioner said and did during these periods of anxiety about the baby's symptoms are retrospective and may well be coloured by the events that followed. The second mother whose baby died before it could be treated in hospital was a vulnerable young girl isolated from her own family and surrounded by hostile in-laws who blamed her for the break up of the husband's first marriage. She was told her baby had croup but when finally an ambulance was called the child died on the way to hospital. The mother had a prolonged grief reaction and projected much of her misery onto the family doctor.

Hospital Admissions

The other two mothers whose babies died of congenital heart disease had formed emotional ties with the nursing staff of the wards to which their babies were repeatedly admitted. They were both deeply grieved by the deaths of the babies but felt that everything possible had been done.

Two other mongol babies were admitted on many occasions in their first year but they both improved considerably in the second year. In these cases, too, the ward staff were regarded as very supportive, so much so that the parents were encouraged to get in touch with the hospital or even to go straight to the ward if they were worried.

One baby had bilateral cataract as an additional congenital anomaly, and by the end of the period of study, he had undergone four operations.

Only one child was admitted to a subnormality hospital for the purpose of "giving his mother a rest". He was admitted twice to the hospital before he was two. After the second admission during which he showed more signs of distress at separation from his mother than on the first occasion, his developmental progress came to a temporary halt and he showed marked separation anxiety. His mother concluded that the admission to give her a rest had produced more problems than it had solved.

Only two of the control babies were admitted to hospital during the period of study. One boy went in for four days with bronchiolitis at the age of one month. He also had a febrile convulsion in his second year but was not then sent into hospital because of the strong family history of febrile convulsions.

A febrile convulsion did lead to admission of a second control child. This little girl had a second admission following a fall off a kitchen stool at home when she hit her head on a drawer. Two hours later she became deeply unconscious and was taken to hospital for an emergency craniotomy. She remained unconscious for four days. Speech returned eleven days after the fall and she was able to walk again four months later.

Other Separation Experiences

Apart from hospital admissions for children or parents, none of the control children were separated from their parents for more than a night. It was quite a common practice, particularly in the second year, for the parents to leave the babies with grandparents overnight. No mother of a control child had a longer holiday away from their child. The mothers who had a subsequent baby were separated from the index child for only forty-eight hours.

The mongols experienced separation, apart from admissions, more frequently. One mother left her baby with a foster mother for three weeks whilst she went on holiday with husband and older child and, in the second year, the same baby was fostered for six weeks whilst the rest of the family were abroad. Another mongol went to stay with his grandparents while the parents had a fortnights holiday. Two of the mongols ceased to have contact with one parent when the marriage broke up and a third was separated from the father for six weeks at a time of marital crisis. As in the control families, the majority of mothers having subsequent children were in hospital for only forty-eight hours but there was one exception in the mongol families where the mother spent eight weeks in hospital awaiting the birth of her second child, whilst the father, with some help from relatives, looked after his mongol son.

Symptoms and Problems

Half the mongol babies were described as having very noisy breathing or persistent grunting in the first year. This noisy breathing was found in children with normal hearts as well as in children with congenital heart disease, and was not a symptom of respiratory distress. Six babies who also had congenital heart disease had attacks of breathlessness, three were also cyanosed even at rest and two others had cyanotic attacks during feeding. The attacks of breathlessness and cyanosis were extremely alarming to the parents. Such symptoms were found in none of the controls but two otherwise healthy babies had febrile convulsions in the second year which was a more alarming experience for the older couple with their first child than it was for a couple whose other child had had similar convulsions and had remained otherwise healthy.

Behaviour problems emerged in some of the children in the second year. Four of the mongol children produced disturbance of behaviour that caused concern to their parents but only one of the controls behaved in such a way that the parents regarded him as being more difficult than other children of his age. The majority of the control children were, by the time they were two years old, "into everything", by which their mothers meant that they were very active, highly inquisitive and required constant watching. None of the mothers of the children described as being "into everything" regarded this behaviour as being anything out of the ordinary and they described their children with a mixture of pride and loving exasperation. Two of the mongol children were undoubtedly hyperkinetic. They had both developed marked overactivity by the age of eighteen months and this continued to the end of the period of study. The mothers gave descriptions of typical behaviour but both children provided abundant evidence of hyperkinetic behaviour on at least two interview visits.

Two of the mongol children had acquired the habit of head banging. One little boy was healthy and had presented no other problems of management in the first two years. The other child who developed this habit was the boy who had bilateral cataract and whose sight was still poor after four operations.

Several mothers of both mongol and control babies described their babies as liking to hurt other people when they were aged between nine and fifteen months. When the behaviour complained of occurred in an interview, it became evident that the babies were only indulging in exploratory play of the sort that most babies do, perhaps learning to distinguish "self" which hurts if pinched and "someone else", which does not hurt but may look cross if pinched. Two mongol children persisted in pinching, hitting and pulling the hair of parents and siblings.

Disruption of Sibling's Play

An inquisitive, crawling baby or toddler is likely to knock over toys and models and to disrupt the games of an older child. At the end of the period of study, equal numbers of mongols and controls were noticeably disruptive of the older siblings' play. The way in which the two groups of babies caused disruption was different as the mongols were more liable to knock or break toys and games whilst the normal child was more inclined to protest at not being allowed to join in. At eighteen months of age the normal controls were much more disruptive of the play of older children than the mongols who were then much less mobile. By the end of the study, some of the control children were learning social behaviour and by that time all but one of the mongols were at least able to propel themselves across a room and could no longer be contained out of the sibling's way.

The Development of the Babies

As would be expected, the mongol babies reached developmental milestones later than did the control babies. The details of the ages at which

Table 6

Milestones[a]

Code	Smiling (in weeks)		Sitting (in months)		Walking (in months)		Words (in months)	
	M	C	M	C	M	C	M	C
1	9	12	9	7	24	11	17	12
2	18	5	12	6	26	18	24	12
3	14	6	12	7	–	15	15	15
4	12	12	14	5	–	12	12	12
5	7	4	12	8	–	14	18	11
6	10	–	Died	–	–	–	–	–
7	8	5	12	8	28	22	24	13
8	9	4	17	8	–	17	–	12
9	8	5	10	7	–	14	–	12
10	14	6	12	9	–	18	22	15
11	12	8	15	5	–	12	27	16
12	16	5	30	8	–	18	–	11
13	8	5	12	7	–	18	9	14
15	8	8	12	7	24	17	24	17
16	9	8	10	11	20	16	13	20
17	12	6	10	6	24	11	12	12
18	12	8	12	10	24	14	21	24
19	12	6	18	6	–	12	14	12
20	12	6	18	7	–	12	15	12
21	12	8	12	7	30	20	36	27
22	6	8	7	7	–	11	8	11
23	14	4	17	6	–	15	–	12
24	10	6	11	6	–	12	13	12
25	16	4	12	8½	–	17½	20	12
26	8	12	12	7	Died	18	–	16
27	20	12	11	5	–	16	18	23
28	5	4	13	9	–	18	–	15
29	9	4	10	7	–	12	12	14
30	6	4	Died	7	–	11	–	12
31	2	4	Died	8	Died	17	–	15

[a] Differences between mongol babies and control babies for all four milestones were significant at 0·001 level. Wilcoxon Matched Pairs-Signed Ranks Test (Siegal, 1959)

four milestones, namely smiling, sitting unsupported, walking and speaking single words, were reached by both groups of babies are shown in Table 6. The later milestones, words and walking, show a wider discrepancy between the two groups than do the earlier milestones of smiling and sitting. Even so there was some overlap in the ages at which the milestones were achieved. Parents' recall of the ages at which developmental milestones are reached is known to be unreliable. Those milestones which are most influenced by observer bias such as smiling and first words are the most unreliable and a more clear cut event such as beginning to walk unaided is at least affected by parental bias.

Some of the mongol babies were not significantly behind the controls in the first year of life. The gap between the groups widens in the second year and is particularly noticeable in walking as no mongol walked before the age of twenty months by which time all but two of the controls were walking.

There was a striking difference by the end of the period of study between the play observed in the two groups of children. Obviously this difference reflects the difference in levels of cognitive and motor development. All but one of the control children were showing clear evidence of imaginative play by their use of toy cars, by putting dolls to bed or by pretending for example to use a telephone or make a cup of tea. However, there was some evidence of imaginative play to be seen in fourteen of the mongols.

Practical Aspects of Care

Physical health as well as motor and cognitive development as demonstrated by achievement of milestones affects the practical care of a child. A mobile child requires more watching than a baby who cannot move but the latter may be more difficult to transport particularly if the family has no car. A child who is difficult to feed can take up much of the mother's time and the child who remains incontinent produces much more washing to be done. In addition, the care of a communicating child may be in some ways easier than the care of a child who can not talk and will certainly be much more rewarding for the mother than the care of an unresponsive child. The scoring of the practical aspects of care for each child in the two groups is to be found in Tables 7–9.

Speech, mobility, feeding and toilet training show marked differences between the mongol children and the controls. The mongol babies were seen as more dependent by their mothers but they were marginally less likely to have tantrums.

Two practical considerations, ease of shopping and availability of baby sitters, have a major effect on the every day lives of parents. The

Table 7
Practical aspects of care

Code	Speech Scale: 1. No contact, no response 2. Understands but no words 3. Single words 4. Simple phrases 5. Talks—not always understood 6. Talks fluently and clearly		Walking 1. Not yet sitting 2. Sits still 3. Crawls 4. Walks 5. Runs, walks and climbs		Mobility 1. Needs carrying everywhere 2. Occasionally has to be carried 3. Rarely carried		Feeding 1. Still uses bottle 2. Bottle as comforter only 3. Strained or tinned food usually 4. Usually family diet. Tins 2 times week 5. Full family diet	
	M	C	M	C	M	C	M	C
1	3	5	4	5	2	3	5	5
2	3	6	5	5	3	2	5	5
3	4	6	3	5	1	3	5	5
4	3	5	4	4	2	2	3	5
7	3	6	4	5	2	3	5	5
8	2	5	3	5	1	3	4	5
9	2	6	3	5	1	3	3	5
10	3	4	3	5	1	3	3	5
11	3	3	3	5	1	2	3	5
12	1	3	3	5	1	3	3	5
13	2	4	3	5	1	3	5	5
15	3	3	3	5	1	3	5	5
16	3	4	4	5	2	3	4	5
17	3	5	4	5	1	2	4	5
18	3	3	5	5	2	3	5	5
19	2	5	2	5	1	3	4	5
20	3	2	2	5	1	3	3	5
21	3	6	4	5	2	3	4	5
22	3	4	3	5	1	3	5	5
23	2	5	3	5	1	2	4	5
24	3	5	3	5	1	3	3	4
25	3	6	3	5	1	3	5	5
26	2	6	3	5	1	3	4	5
27	2	3	3	5	1	3	3	5
28	1	3	1	4	1	2	4	4
29	3	3	3	4	1	2	4	5

Table 8
Practical aspects of care

Code	Baby sitting Scale: 1. Never have baby sitter 2. Baby sitting is a problem 3. No problems with baby sitters		Shopping 1. Never take X shopping 2. Major difficulties 3. Minor difficulties 4. No problems		Physical health 1. Always a matter of concern 2. More of a problem than for other children 3. Some worries but no more than others 4. No problems		Hospital visits 1. Attend hospital clinic regularly 2. Do not attend hospital clinic	
	M	C	M	C	M	C	M	C
1	3	2	3	4	4	3	1	2
2	3	3	4	4	4	3	2	2
3	3	2	2	4	3	3	1	2
4	3	2	4	3	3	2	1	1
7	3	3	3	3	3	3	2	2
8	3	1	4	4	3	3	2	2
9	3	3	4	3	3	3	1	2
10	2	3	2	4	1	4	1	2
11	3	3	4	4	2	3	1	2
12	1	3	2	3	2	4	1	2
13	3	3	2	4	3	4	1	2
15	3	3	4	1	3	4	2	2
16	3	3	3	4	2	4	1	2
17	2	2	3	2	3	4	1	2
18	2	2	3	4	3	2	1	1
19	3	3	4	3	4	4	2	2
20	2	3	1	4	2	3	1	2
21	3	3	4	4	2	3	1	2
22	3	3	4	3	3	3	1	2
23	2	2	4	3	3	4	1	2
24	2	1	4	4	4	1	1	2
25	3	3	2	3	3	3	1	2
26	3	3	4	4	1	3	1	2
27	3	3	4	4	2	4	1	2
28	3	2	3	4	3	2	2	2
29	3	3	4	4	3	4	1	2

Table 9

Practical aspects of care

Code	Independence Scale: 1. Completely dependent 2. More dependent than most at his age 3. About same as other children 4. Very independent		Tantrums 1. Never 2. Infrequent 3. Frequent but short 4. Frequent and long		Playgroup/nursery 1. Already attending 2. Name down 3. Vague intention 4. Not intended to go		Toilet training 1. Not attempted 2. Attempted training 3. Clean and dry	
	M	C	M	C	M	C	M	C
1	3	4	1	3	2	3	3	2
2	3	3	2	3	1	2	2	3
3	1	4	2	1	1	2	2	3
4	2	3	3	2	1	1	2	2
7	2	4	2	2	1	2	2	3
8	2	4	3	2	2	2	1	2
9	2	4	3	3	1	2	1	3
10	2	3	2	3	1	2	1	2
11	2	3	1	2	1	2	1	3
12	1	3	3	2	1	1	1	3
13	2	4	2	2	3	4	1	2
15	3	4	1	2	4	4	1	2
16	2	3	1	3	2	1	2	2
17	3	3	3	·3	3	2	2	2
18	3	3	3	3	1	2	2	3
19	2	4	1	3	3	2	2	3
20	2	3	1	1	2	3	1	2
21	2	4	2	1	1	1	2	3
22	2	4	2	2	1	3	1	2
23	2	3	2	2	1	2	1	3
24	2	4	2	2	3	3	1	2
25	2	4	1	3	1	2	2	3
26	2	3	1	1	2	2	1	2
27	2	4	1	1	4	3	1	2
28	2	4	1	3	1	2	1	1
29	3	4	3	3	3	3	1	1

mongol babies were not more difficult when taken shopping than were the control babies in the second year of the follow up. Baby sitters were found to be as willing to come and sit with a mongol baby as they were to sit with a normal baby. In both groups of families, relatives most frequently acted as baby sitters, but even those mothers of mongols who had no relative in the area usually had a neighbour who was happy to take over in order to give the parents an evening out together. One mother of a mongol baby had not told her elderly mother or neighbours of the child's handicap. She never asked anyone to baby sit, had not been out with her husband for nine years, and had never had anyone to sit for her elder children who were aged nine and seven at the birth of the mongol.

Big differences are seen in the physical health as perceived by the mother and also in the number of hospital out-patient visits. Most of the families with mongol babies found that keeping the out-patient appointments was a problem as it was not always easy to arrange transport. In many cases the father had to arrange to take a day or half a day off work with a corresponding loss of money.

4 First News of the Handicap

In the course of the first exploratory study (Gath, 1972b) of families of children with two different types of congenital malformations, the mothers were asked how they had first learnt of the child's disability. This study was carried out in 1970 and the subjects were ten-year-old children with mongolism and their families, and ten-year-old children with cleft palate/cleft lip and their families. The age of the affected children meant that the mothers were recalling the experience of being told of the handicap as it had happened ten years before. Not only would their accounts be inaccurate due to loss of memory but subsequent events would introduce a further bias. Nonetheless, it was evident that many of the twenty mothers interviewed during that study still had bitter feelings at the way in which they had learnt that their child was a mongol. The views expressed by the mothers of the mongol children were in marked contrast to those of the majority of the mothers of children with cleft lip/cleft palate. Where there was a possibility of an operation to correct the deformity, parents were cheered by the surgeons practice of bringing before and after photographs. Subsequent events in which the surgeons demonstrated their ability to keep their promise to make the child look normal, or very nearly normal, had also coloured the accounts of how the mothers had first learnt of the deformity, but the bias in this case was in the opposite direction to that affecting the recalled memories of the mothers of mongols.

Since 1960, in which year most of the mothers referred to above were told of their child's handicap, there has been more attention given to the effect of the way in which parents are told the news (Franklin, 1963) and to studies of how and when it is best accomplished (Drillien and Wilkinson, 1964; D'Arcy, 1968; Berg *et al.*, 1969; Carr, 1970). All the studies lead to the conclusion that more parents who were told early were satisfied than were those who were told later and there is little support for the idea that doctors should delay telling parents that they have an abnormal new born child in order to allow them first to become attached to the child. Uncertainty was likely to breed further anguish for the parents and denial of a defect later admitted was the most damaging, producing long lasting resentment. There is no indication from published studies that telling a mother of her baby's congenital abnormality soon after the birth was likely to precipitate a serious psychiatric breakdown in the puerperium as had been feared in the past.

The National Association for Mental Health (1971), considered the findings of these studies and produced some guidelines. The advice given to those who have to perform this most delicate task of speaking to the parents is in accord with the views expressed nearly twenty years before by Kanner (1953) and with the conclusions drawn by Wolfensberger (1968) in his extensive review of the literature. Perhaps the most important point made is that breaking the news must not be considered as an event in isolation and must be "only the first step in the continuing management of the child".

The working party set up by the National Association for Mental Health reported about half way through the period in which the sample of mongols in the main propective study was being collected.

Who Tells the Parents

As has been described in Chapter 2, the mongol babies were born in all parts of the area of the then Regional Hospital Board involving five main medical centres and eleven different paediatricians. Up to publication of the working party's report there was little information to guide doctors, and handling the situation of the congenitally abnormal child varied from centre to centre and even from paediatrician to paediatrician within centres. There was also some disagreement as to where the responsibility lay. Some doctors believed that the obstetrician who had looked after the woman during pregnancy should be the person to tell her of the outcome. Others regarded the child and the diagnosis of abnormality to be a purely paediatric concern and that the paediatrician should tell the parents of his finding and his opinion. Still others quite rightly considered the problem to be one which affected all the family and that the family doctor should be involved from the start.

In this series no parent was told by an obstetrician.

Twenty-two mothers (73%) were first told of their babies' abnormality by a paediatrician. The timing and setting varied. Some were told whilst they were still in the maternity ward, others at an out-patient clinic appointment and a third group were told in their own homes when the paediatrician made a domicillary visit (Table 10). All the domicillary visits were made by a consultant paediatrician and in two of the three instances in out-patients the news was broken by a consultant

Table 10

Parents told of diagnosis by paediatrician

| | Time after birth of baby | | |
	Within 1 week	After 1 week	TOTAL
In hospital	9	7	16
As out-patients	0	3	3
In their own home	1	2	3
TOTAL	10	12	22

Parents told of diagnosis by general practitioner
Time after birth of baby

	Within 1 week	After 1 week	TOTAL
In G.P. maternity unit	2	0	2
After hospital birth	0	3	3
With paediatrician doing domicillary visit next day	2	0	2
G.P. telling wife later	0	1	1
TOTAL			8

paediatrician. In hospital the news was most likely to be broken by a less experienced paediatrician, usually of registrar grade. Half the parents were told by a resident paediatrician, other than the consultant whom they met later.

Although it has been stressed by some paediatricians that the setting is important to parents, the meaning of being told at home or in hospital was overshadowed by the importance of the timing of the news. Two sets of parents were told when the father had arrived to take his wife and new baby home. In both cases, the father had been visiting his wife regularly in hospital and neither couple had suspected anything was wrong until they had been on the point of taking their child home. In both cases, the parents resented strongly the time that was chosen to tell them that the baby was not considered normal. Both mothers had dressed the baby for the first time in the baby clothes they had made or bought during the pregnancy and they were eager to take the child home, to see him amongst all the preparations they had made and to show him to friends, neighbours and relatives. One couple, who had been told at the point of departure from hospital, left the baby behind and then returned home without him to spend an agonizing week of dis-cussion and indecision before they came back to take the child into the family home. The other couple did take their baby home as planned but they then kept her hidden away for six weeks from relatives and friends before they could bring themselves to acknowledge the gifts and letters of congratulations that had arrived during the week the mother and child had been in hospital after the birth.

On three occasions, the paediatrician and general practitioner worked together to tell the parents. Two general practitioners had delivered the baby at home and, as soon as they suspected that the child was a mongol, they asked the paediatrician to make a domicillary visit. Both these doctors first told the parents that they were worried about the new-born child and explained the reason for their concern. The paediatrician, who came within twenty-four hours in both cases, confirmed the general practitioners' suspicions and was able to offer more information as well as a definite diagnosis to the parents. In contrast to the paediatrician and general practitioner working in partnership with both parents, there was one case when the parents were told separately by different people. The father was first told by himself by the paediatric registrar when he came to collect his wife and baby. This man had been worried about the possibility of a mongol ever since his wife had become pregnant at the age of forty. He had also noticed that the baby did indeed have mongoloid features shortly after birth but when this was denied by the obstetric house officer, he was reassured and believed his child then to be normal. The mother had been in hospital for two months before the birth of the baby with hypertension and, for this reason, it was decided that she should not be told until later. The father found the denial and then the news that his fears had been justified, coupled with the instructions not to tell his wife, put him under intolerable strain. The wife who was told by her general practitioner a week later was equally critical of the way in which the breaking of the news was handled. Both husband and wife were distressed that they should have been deceived and then so clumsily handled by the hospital who "should have known us after I had been in so long".

Five general practitioners handled the task of telling the parents on their own. In two instances, the babies were born in general practitioner maternity units and so the man on the spot was the family doctor. In two further cases, particular family doctors volunteered to tell the parents as they had a particular knowledge of that family. One general practitioner had known the family in a village in a very rural area for many years and was regarded by them as an old friend. The parents appreciated this relationship despite the pain that the news brought them. One young couple had just moved and the old family doctor who had known the wife from childhood travelled to their new home to see them. Although their initial reaction was "We knew something was wrong when we saw it was him", this couple too were glad to be told by someone who knew them and who obviously cared about them.

The last general practitioner case was one of the only two about which there was doubt in the diagnosis. The baby had minimal physical signs of classic Down's syndrome, even though every cell showed the characteristic chromosomal trisomy 21. The parents were told three weeks after the birth that a blood test was necessary and they were told of the definite diagnosis when the child was six weeks old. This couple whose marriage was in a precarious state even before the pregnancy was established parted when the father refused to accept the child once he had been labelled as a mongol.

Two general practitioners were described by their patients as being particularly supportive after the news had been broken to the parents in hospital. Although not actually breaking the news, these doctors played an important part in helping the parents through the initial phase of shock.

One Parent Told Alone

Six mothers were told of the diagnosis at a time when they did not have their husbands with them. In each case, these women had to go home and break the news to their husbands. One of these women was told on the second day after the birth of her daughter because she suspected mongolism. She particularly requested to be allowed to tell her husband herself. He had had a previous history of psychiatric disorder, including a period as an in-patient not long before the birth. The family doctor was somewhat apprehensive about his reaction but his wife knew how to approach him and together they coped well with the shock.

Four of the other mothers were told by themselves as they were in the habit of visiting the hospital alone with the traditional attitude that the children were "women's work". Three of these women had little support at any time from their husbands but the fourth couple had a much warmer relationship despite their rather rigid roles.

Only one couple were distressed that the mother had been told at a time when her husband was not with her. This marriage later broke up and, in the first few months after his wife had deserted him, the father reproached himself for not having been present at the time when his wife had had most need of him.

Only one father was told and then asked not to tell his wife. As has been described, he found this situation put him under immense strain. He could get no comfort himself and was deeply distressed at having to deceive his wife.

When the Parents Were Told

When the parents later talked about their experience of hearing about the baby's abnormality, they were much more concerned about when they had been told than by whom or where they had been told. Thirteen couples (43%) clearly understood by the end of the first week after the birth of their baby that the child had Down's syndrome or was "a mongol". Seven couples (23%) said that they did not know for certain what was wrong with the child until after the baby was six weeks old.

No attempt was made in this study to ask either the paediatricians or the general practitioners for their versions of the interview in which the news was broken. There is likely to be a considerable discrepancy between the accounts of the same event from doctor and parent since both versions are open to bias. It is probable that in several cases an attempt was made to tell the parents earlier than they later remembered, but it is frequent in emotionally charged situations for the parents not to understand or remember all that they are told (Davies *et al.*, 1972). It is, however, the subjective experiences of the parents and what remains in their minds after the interview that influences family attitudes and not the objective date or accurate description of the interview.

How the Parents Felt About the Way They Were Told

Eight (27%) of the couples said that they were satisfied with the way they had been given the information that their child was a mongol.

Twelve couples (40%) were definitely not satisfied. Ten (33%) were not able to express views either way as most of them felt that the impact of the news was such that it could not have been modified by any alteration in the way it was broken. The two fathers who reacted by rejecting the child after learning of the diagnosis were in this last group. Both of them considered that no amount of skill or kindness could have lessened the shock of the news. Neither the father who rejected his child permanently nor the younger man who returned to the family after six weeks discussed the child with a doctor or social worker after the initial interview, although both were very willing to talk over their experiences and their feelings with the research worker, a few weeks later.

Another father, who had initially sworn to the paediatrician who had told him, later said he did not think that he would have behaved differently if he had been approached in another way. His wife agreed that his reaction would probably have been just as vigorous if he had been told at a different time or in a different place or by a different person. This couple had long standing problems of communication between each other, neighbours and workmates.

Although five times as many couples who were definitely not satisfied

Table 11

Degree of satisfaction and who told the parents

	Paediatrician	General practitioner	TOTAL
Satisfied	6	2	8
Unable to say	6	2	10
Not satisfied	10	2	12
TOTAL	22	8	30

$X^2 = 1.52$ n.s.

with the way they had been told of the diagnosis had been told by a hospital paediatrician as opposed to a family doctor, there is no significant correlation between who told the parents about the baby's condition and the degree of satisfaction (Table 11). Some who had been told by their own family doctors were pleased that this delicate task had been left to someone who knew them well. On the other hand, one woman regarded it as definitely unfair that the hospital doctors "who knew all along" had left the general practitioner to break it to her. Most frequently satisfied were those whose family doctors and the paediatrician had both been involved, particularly where there had been a home delivery and the paediatrician had visited the next day in the company of their own doctor.

All but one of the parents who were satisfied with the way they had been told the news had been told in the first week (Table 12). Degree of definite dissatisfaction increased with the lapse of time between the birth and the definite diagnosis being made to the parents. There is a less striking difference between those told very late, after six weeks, and those told between one and six weeks than there is between those told in the first week and all those told later. There is a marked difference be-

Table 12

Degree of satisfaction and timing of breaking the news

	Time after birth of baby			
	Early Within 1 week	Later 1 to 6 weeks	Very late After 6 weeks	TOTAL
Satisfied	7	1	0	8
Unable to say	3	5	2	10
Not satisfied	3	4	5	12
TOTAL	13	10	7	30

$X^2 = 10.48$, d.f. $= 4$, p < 0.05

Table 13

Degree of satisfaction and timing of breaking the news

| | Time after birth of baby | | |
	Early Within 1 week	Late After 1 week	TOTAL
Satisfied	7	1	8
Unable to say or definitely not satisfied	6	1	22
TOTAL	13	17	30
$X^2 = 6.39$, p < 0.05			

tween those who were definitely satisfied at the way the matter had been handled and those who could not say or were dissatisfied in the timing of the news (Table 13).

Even so, the parents who were told early and were dissatisfied still mentioned delay, evasion or denial as the prime cause for their dissatisfaction. Typical of the comments was "I don't see why we had to force the information out. I think this upset me more than anything else—this sort of dreadful cover-up".

Over a third of the mothers had realized something was definitely wrong with the baby when they first saw it. Others were puzzled by extra attention or by nurses crowding round the cot. In two cases, it was the father who noticed first. One father and one mother kept their suspicions to themselves, not even sharing them with the other parent because, as one said "If by any chance I had been wrong, I would have worried someone else unnecessarily".

Resentment at delay at being told or evasion was particularly strong when the child had been in hospital for some weeks and the diagnosis had not been in doubt. One baby had been in hospital six weeks. The mother's comments were:

They really knew themselves but they waited their time to tell us. Now why couldn't we have been told then? We were going up there three or four times a week to see him and we were told the day we went to fetch him, and that I strongly resent.

Where there was genuine difficulty in diagnosis, the parents were much less resentful and more appreciative of the difficulty in some cases of making a definite diagnosis before chromosome studies could be done. The wait for the results of the genetic investigations was distressing. One family were told first that it was unlikely that their baby was a mongol, only to be told later that the chromosome investigation had shown that he was. All the others had been told the child was definitely a mongol or very likely to be one when the blood samples were taken, except in those cases when blood was taken only from the child in hospital and not from the parents.

Breach of trust following evasion or a denial had a lasting effect on the relationship between doctors and patients. One family doctor was requested not to tell his patient about her mongol baby by the paediatrician. In the closely knit rural community in which the family lived, it became apparent after a few weeks that everyone appeared to know except the parents themselves. The grandparents were told by another doctor in the practice who did not know that the parents had not been fully informed. What no one realized was that the parents themselves had suspected that the child was a mongol right from the start. The mother found her tentative questions were met with silence or a quick change of subject. Finally she asked her own doctor outright and he arranged a domicillary visit from the consultant paediatrician that evening. The general practitioner himself was distressed and embarrassed at not being able to treat the family in his customary frank way, and later told the wife that there had been many times when he had wished he could have told her.

Undoubtedly the parents project much of their grief upon the people who are present and involved with them when they first learn the distressing news that their child has a lasting disability. This fact, however, does not detract from the findings in this study showing that evasions and postponements breed mistrust. In particular, it is initial denial that anything is seriously wrong that is particularly likely to destroy any vestige of a therapeutic relationship between the doctor and the family.

It is obvious that the most experienced doctor will not always be on hand whenever a baby with congenital malformation is born or when parents first become worried about their child. Passage of time is very slow to parents in their initial distress. The results indicate that if the paediatrician does regard this situation as an emergency and sees the parents as soon as possible, he will be in a better position to continue advising and supporting them than someone who comes to be regarded as having deceived them or treated them "like nincompoops".

The findings of this part of the study support the ideas behind the recommendations of the National Association for Mental Health Working Party. Clearly expressed advice on how to handle the problems of deformed and abnormal babies is presented by Davies et al., 1972. The suggestion that the doctors should tell "the truth and nothing but the truth but not necessarily the whole truth all at once" is a useful guideline, as more hard and fast rules will not be adequate in every case.

5 The Effect Upon the Health of the Parents

The question of whether the care of a severely mentally handicapped child will impair the health of the parents has aroused some controversy. Thirty years ago, paediatricians were in little doubt that the inevitable result of the responsibility for such a child was the increasing exhaustion of the mother. Parents were advised to find a place for their severely handicapped child in an institution as soon as possible (Aldrich, 1947). The medical advisers were so confident that this was the only reasonable course of action that it was not a rare occurrence for arrangements to be made for admission of the baby to a long stay hospital without consulting the mother and sometimes without even allowing her to see the baby. The advocates of immediate removal of the handicapped child from the family have produced only scanty and largely anecdotal evidence of the alleged inevitable ill effects on the mothers' health. Their policy of shielding the mother from the sight of the new born defective child could produce profound distress later on when it was found that the infant had not grown up as the monster that had been feared (Farrell, 1956).

The initial reaction of any parent to the birth of a child with any defect is grief, vividly and movingly described by Brinkworth and Collins (1969). Brinkworth is himself the parent of two handicapped children. The grief reaction is in some ways similar to that of bereavement when a child dies (Solnit and Stark, 1961) but unlike a death in the family, the continued presence of the handicapped child will be a constant reminder to the parents of their loss. Now that families are small and, to some degree, planned, a normal, healthy baby is confidently expected to arrive at the end of the pregnancy. When instead an abnormal child is born, the parents may mourn the normal child who had existed in their fantasy throughout pregnancy and regard the real, defective child as an intruder usurping the fantasy child's place or as "a living grave of a hoped for normal baby" (Goldie, 1966).

During the first weeks and months following the realization of the handicap the parents have to experience grief and hopefully resolve it. They then must cope with two other adjustments, one in which they have to refashion their hopes and aspirations for this particular child and the other in which they have to tackle the every day practical reality of coping with a handicapped child. Wolfensberger (1968) refers to the three stages of parental adjustment as the initial shock, the value crisis and the reality crisis.

There is no doubt that many if not all parents go through the stage of shock and grief, but very little is known of how they cope with the second stage of the change of aspirations for the child. That some parents do not pass easily through this stage is indicated by the common behaviour of "shopping around" for yet another medical panacea which may have the magic power of cure. More data is available on the effects on parents of the practical problems of caring for a handicapped child.

Marked effects on the parents' health were described by Holt (1957) and Schonell and Watts (1957). Holt, studying two hundred and seven families with a severely subnormal child living at home in Sheffield, found that 19% of the mothers were exhausted by the emotional stress and by the physical work involved in the daily care of such a child. Similar findings in fifty Australian families with a subnormal child were reported by Schonell and Watts. In both studies the health of the mother was described as being in constant jeopardy and fathers too were said to be suffering, although to a lesser extent.

These gloomy findings refer to families who were provided with very inadequate social, and educational support in their task of bringing up their affected children. Both the studies quoted can be criticized for their lack of comparison with families with normal children living in similar socio-economic circumstances. Very different results were reported by Caldwell and Guze (1960) in America who found that the mental health of mothers of children living at home but regularly attending a clinic was not significantly different from that of mothers of similar children in an institution.

Other investigators have used self-administered inventories to compare the mental health of mothers of mentally handicapped children with mothers of emotionally disturbed or physically ill children (Erikson, 1969; Cummings, 1966). The findings that neurotic symptoms are much more common in mothers of mentally handicapped children are interpreted as meaning that the symptoms represent a reaction to the strain of looking after such a child.

Little attempt has been made to relate the detrimental effects on parents' health to the difference between the amount of care required by the handicapped child and that needed by a normal child of the same age. The thirty mongol babies in this study have not been shown to be very much more difficult to care for than were the normal babies. Certain individual babies were very difficult, and even frightening, to feed in the first few months. These babies were those with severe symptoms of congenital heart disease, some of whom would become very breathless and cyanosed in the midst of a feed. In some respects, the mongol babies were no more of a problem than the normal babies and they were less likely to be demanding and disruptive in the small hours. By the end of the study, the increased mobility of the normal babies made them more liable to falls or other accidents and more likely to be destructive or a nuisance to other members of the family.

Previous Health of the Parents

The parents of the mongol babies were slightly older than the parents of the control babies. Despite this difference in age, mongol parents had not experienced more ill health prior to the birth of the index baby.

Thirteen mothers in each group had been previously admitted to hospital. Surgery for common, relatively minor conditions accounted for the admissions of six of the control women and of two of the mothers of mongols. Two mongols mothers had short admissions to medical wards for investigation, one for migraine and the other for recurrent urinary infection. One control mother had been investigated for anaemia. The two groups of mothers showed a similar pattern of chronic illness. Two women, one in each group, had sanatorium treatment for tuberculosis as teenagers and both made a complete recovery. Two other mothers, again one in each group, had chronic infections involving long periods of hospital treatment and repeated operations in childhood, for osteomyelitis in one case and bronchiectasis in the other. Another mongol mother had ulcerative colitis which had been very troublesome up to the time of her marriage. She had brief relapses following the births of her two previous children.

It is reasonable to suppose that gynaecological problems with more difficulty in becoming pregnant would account partly for the difference in age between the two groups of women. Yet the mothers of the mongol children did not have more gynaecological problems than the mothers of the normal children, as three mothers in each group had been treated by gynaecologists. Two mothers of mongol babies had previous miscarriages but three of the control mothers had miscarriages or a still birth before the birth of the study baby. Two mothers of mongols had sought advice specifically about their infertility as had one mother of a normal baby. One mother who later gave birth to a mongol had experienced a previous pregnancy that ended with the formation of a hydatidiform mole.

There is no evidence to suggest that the mothers of the mongol babies were more susceptible to psychiatric illness than were the mothers of the normal babies. No mother who later gave birth to a mongol had consulted a doctor about depressive or "nervous" symptoms, but two women who were to have normal babies had out-patient treatment for depression, one in the first year of marriage and the other following the birth of a previous baby.

The health records of the fathers followed a similar pattern to that of the mothers. Ten fathers of mongol babies and twelve fathers of control babies had undergone hospital treatment. As with the mothers, surgery for relatively minor complaints, including appendicitis, accounted for three admissions of mongol fathers and five admissions of control fathers. Trauma accounted for treatment required by two fathers of mongols and by two fathers of control babies. The two control fathers had minor injuries requiring overnight admission, both involving fractured clavicles, one of which had been incurred playing football and the other in a motor bicycle accident. The trauma suffered by the two mongol fathers was more serious and were, in both cases, industrial accidents with associated problems of compensation. These two men had suffered back injuries for which they received treatment for more than a year. Since their accidents, they had continued to have pain from their injuries and were both forced to take poorly paid light work. Two fathers of control babies had out-patient treatment in the eye department of the general hospital for chronic eye complaints.

Examples of what are usually considered as psychosomatic disorders were found in the past medical history of men in both groups. Two fathers from families with a mongol baby had had duodenal ulcers in the past and two control fathers had had asthma. One of the asthmatic fathers still had symptoms at the time of the birth of the study baby but asthma had never prevented him from going to work.

Two fathers of mongol babies had previous admissions to psychiatric hospitals. One of these two was admitted for four days only, suffering from an acute anxiety state. This admission occurred four years before the birth of the mongol child but he had remained very prone to anxiety, particularly in relation to stress at work. He had, however, managed to function well with surveillance and occasional tranquillizers from a vigilant and supportive family doctor.

The other man had been admitted with manic depressive psychosis before marriage. One of the fathers of normal babies also had a history of psychiatric treatment for anxiety.

From the past medical records there is no evidence to indicate that the parents of the mongol babies in the study were a particularly vulnerable group. Despite the control parents being slightly younger than the parents of mongol babies there are very similar patterns of past illness in the two groups.

Questionnaire Findings

The finding that the parents of the mongol babies can not be regarded as more vulnerable than the parents of the controls is supported by the results of the Eysenck Personality Inventory which was completed by both groups of parents. There was no significant difference between the mean scores of the mothers in the two groups or between that of the fathers, neither did the mean scores of fathers or mothers in either group differ from the population mean.

A third bare-line measure of the parents' health was the "Malaise Inventory" a short questionnaire with many items derived from the Cornell Medical Index. This inventory was used in the Isle of Wight to study parents of nine- and ten-year-old children (Rutter *et al.*, 1970). The design of the inventory aims to highlight subjective feelings of ill health and may be said to measure the "grumble factor". The mean scores of the mothers in the two groups were very similar but that of the mongol fathers was slightly higher than that of control fathers.

Follow-up Health Data

Retrospective data of experience of ill health is inevitably open to bias. Throughout the follow up period with five or six interviews, data about the health of each member of the family was collected at every interview. Following the general introductory question "and how has so-and-so been since my last visit?", precise questions were asked about days off work, visits to the general practitioners, clinics or hospitals. Each time, checks were made with the previous interview data to prevent overlapping or double recording of data. Routine post-natal examinations for mothers were excluded as were visits to a doctor for contraceptive advice or supplies.

Use of Medical Services During Period of Study

There was no significant difference in the use of the medical services between the two groups of parents in the two years of follow up, as can be seen in Table 14.

More than half (65% of the total) of the parents made no contact with their general practitioners or hospital services. There is thus no

Table 14

Parents health since birth of index baby
(General practitioner and hospital contacts)

| | Parents | |
	Mongols	Controls
Fathers		
No medical contacts	18	19
All medical contacts	12	11
G.P. only	7	5
Hospital out-patients	0	4
Hospital in-patients	5	2
Mothers		
No medical contacts	16	20
All medical contacts	14	10
G.P. only	9	7
Hospital out-patients	1	1
Hospital in-patients	4	2

evidence of the "inevitable" ill effects on patients' health in the first two years.

Slightly more mothers of mongol babies made use of medical services than did mothers of normal, control babies. This small increase is evident in both general practitioners treatment and hospital in-patient treatment. No one type of medical complaint predominated as physical, psychiatric and gynaecological complaints were all slightly more frequent in mothers of mongols. All the differences, however, are small.

Physical ill health

Physical ill health was slightly more common among control fathers but fathers of mongol children had more psychiatric illness. Not surprisingly some of the parents were still suffering from conditions that had troubled them before the birth of the index baby. One of the men who had had a serious industrial accident had severe headaches and back pain for which he was treated by his general practitioner with the loss of six weeks work. One of the sufferers from chronic eye complaints in the control group had a recurrence which necessitated several visits to the eye hospital. The mildly asthmatic father continued to wheeze periodically. The mother who had migraine before her mongol daughter was born also continued to have attacks but they were no more frequent nor more severe than before. The mother with ulcerative colitis had a relapse after the mongol baby was born. This relapse was more severe than those occurring after the births of her other children but the symptoms were much less severe than they had been before her marriage. Chronic physical illnesses thus flared up again but not more severely than before the birth of the baby and no more frequently in parents of mongol babies than in parents of normal babies.

Psychiatric ill health

The two fathers of mongol children who had previous psychiatric illnesses broke down again within eighteen months of the baby's birth, as did the only control father who had a history of psychiatric illness. Three other fathers of mongols had psychiatric symptoms in the follow-up period. Two of these men had anxiety with depression and the third had anxiety with sexual problems, including impotence and loss of libido. One control father had a mild depressive illness and another a moderately severe anxiety state. Psychiatric illness was slightly more common in fathers of mongol babies but the fathers of normal babies were by no means exempt. The only suicide attempt in the group of parents as a whole was an overdose taken by a nineteen-year-old mother in the control group who was in despair at her seemingly unending housing problems. Housing was a major problem for one mongol family and two of the control families.

The crude signs of ill health as measured by days off work, visits to general practitioners, out-patient treatment or hospital admission reveal no difference between parents in the mongol and control group. During the course of the series of interviews, however, more mongol mothers were seen to be overtly depressed, although they did not at any time consult a doctor about their mood disturbance. The depression was regarded by these women as being an understandable "normal" reaction to the circumstances and, as they did not believe a doctor could remedy the basic cause, they saw no reason to consult one. The four mothers of mongols found to be clinically depressed at their interviews attributed their symptoms to their grief and anxiety over the affected child. The one depressed control mother was another victim of housing problems. When these women are included with the women who went to their doctors with symptoms, the ten (33%) of mothers of mongol babies had depression during the first eighteen months after the birth of the study baby, twice as many as did of the control mothers.

Specific symptoms

An attempt was made to determine how many parents had symptoms at the fifth interview which was carried out between eighteen months and two years after the birth of the baby. Nine questions were asked at this interview.

1. Do you have difficulty getting to sleep at night?
2. Do you wake earlier than you need in the morning?
3. Do you feel tired all the time?
4. How do you feel generally?
5. Are your moods inclined to vary?
6. Have you been feeling depressed?
7. Do you have frequent headaches?
8. Have you been suffering from stomach pain?
9. Have you been getting breathless recently?

All these symptoms with the exception of early waking were more common in mothers of mongol babies than in mothers of normal babies. Early waking, in this case, was not an indicator of mood disturbance but more likely a habit acquired as the normal were more demanding at night, needing middle of the night feeds until a later age and also requiring earlier morning feeds.

There was little difference in the symptoms experienced by the two groups of fathers at this stage, except that there was a tendency for fathers to be more tired and irritable if their child was a mongol.

The General Health Questionnaire

The General Health Questionnaire (Goldberg, 1972) was designed for the detection of non-psychotic psychiatric illness in adult populations and was used at the end of the period of study. Neither the mean scores of the two groups of fathers nor the mean scores of the two groups of mothers were significantly different but mothers of mongols tended to have a higher score than mothers of controls. The grief reactions and depressions suffered by the mongol mothers are either not all detected by this sort of questionnaire or they had resolved to some degree by this time. Certainly all the mothers found to be depressed at one or more interviews had improved by the time subsequent interviews took place.

Conclusions

Recognizable psychiatric illness in the parents does not appear to be related to specific factors in the child. It was not, for example, more common when a child had severe hypotonia or floppiness, which was regarded by Penrose as associated with a prognosis of a severe degree of retardation. Nor was psychiatric illness more common when the child had congenital heart disease as an additional handicap or had pronounced behaviour or management problems. Mothers who already had normal children were no less likely to become depressed than were mothers of first babies. Older mothers were no more vulnerable than those who were still in their twenties. Depression was not more likely to follow an unplanned or surprise pregnancy than one particularly desired.

During the period covered by this study, the first couple of years following the birth of the mongol baby, detrimental effects on parents' health are certainly not inevitable. There is not an increased demand for medical services following the birth of an abnormal baby. There is, however, some evidence that mothers particularly may suffer, not from effects of the extra care demanded by the mongol baby, but from the emotional stress stemming from the profound disappointment and grief mixed with anxiety about the future. These findings are very similar to those reported by Freeston (1971) from his work on the parents of babies with spina bifida. The grief experienced by all parents confronted with serious abnormality in the new born child is usually resolved in the first two years. However, a substantial minority of the parents are unable to recover from grief which may persist as a depression not necessarily known to the family doctor, or as more isolated symptoms indicative of mood disturbance.

6 The Effect on the Marital Relationship of the Parents

Marital disharmony as a result of the stress of bringing up a child with mental handicap has been described in many studies. The most detailed investigations of the marital relationship of parents of a retarded child are by Farber (1959) and Farber and Jenné (1963). This group of workers devised a scale which they called the Farber Index of Marital Integration which was designed to measure how far the husband and wife were in agreement on rank ordering of domestic values. They found that mentally handicapped boys, particularly over the age of nine years, had a more disruptive effect than girls on the relationship between the parents but that this difference was only significant in the families of unskilled or semi-skilled workers. It was also found that placement of the retarded boy in an institution tended to have a beneficial effect on the parents relationship. Fowle (1969), however, using the Farber Index was unable to find any significant difference in marital integration between parents caring for a mentally handicapped child at home, and parents with a similar child in an institution. Farber's studies are exceptional because they represent an attempt to study the marital relationship between the parents by objective measures rather than by reliance on assessment of the state of the relationship from subjective impressions which were usually only obtained from the mother.

In the studies by Holt (1957) and Schonell and Watts (1957), parental quarrelling is described. The incidence (6%) of frequent parental quarrelling in Holt's series needs to be interpreted with care, as there was no control group. Dominian (1968) quoted a figure of between 8 and 14% of all marriages as being the proportion that deteriorate so far as to give serious consideration to separation.

In our survey of one-hundred-and-four families with a mongol child of average age of eight and with at least one other child in the family currently attending a normal school, only three homes were found to be broken by divorce or separation, less than half the expected rate of 7%. Many parents who had written letters to accompany their survey forms described their relationship as strengthened by the presence of the handicapped child. A similar finding was made by Stone (1972) who studied Glasgow families with mongol children. An earlier study by Kramm (1963) of fifty mothers of mongols quotes twenty-one of these mothers as saying that their mongol child had had the effect of drawing husband and wife closer together. In contrast, more broken marriages, varying between 20 and 30%, are found in the families of children institutionalized from before reaching school age, in subnormality hospitals in the same area around Oxford from which the sibling survey sample of mongol children living at home was drawn.

The birth of a baby with an obvious physical deformity may also have an adverse effect on the marriage of the parents. In their study of the families of children with spina bifida in South Wales, Tew et al. (1974) found that the quality of the marital relationship in their index families deteriorated over the years and that the divorce rate was twice that of controls and of the national average.

Recently it has been shown that less dramatic departures from normality in a new born baby can have an adverse effect on the marital relationship. Leiderman (1974) described an increase in the rate of divorce or separation in parents after the birth of a premature baby who had to be nursed in a special care nursery.

The part of the interview schedule from which measures of the marital relationship are made has been used on previous occasions in the Isle of Wight (Rutter et al., 1970) and more recently with families of autistic children and of children with specific developmental receptive language disorder (Cox et al., 1975). The method essentially is based on asking about precise events in a specified length of time. Parents are asked about quarrels in the past three months, about how they come to decisions with examples, about how they apportion the household chores and how they spend their evenings with particular attention to the previous week. The number of hostile, critical or positive remarks throughout the interview are counted and overall ratings of warmth and hostility are made. The development of this interview technique to study family relationships and interactions is described by Brown and Rutter (1966), and Quinton et al. (1976).

The marital data interview was included in the fourth interview of the follow up series of six in this study. It took place one year after the initial interview at a time when the babies were aged between fourteen months and twenty-seven months, as the oldest child to be enrolled was fifteen months when first seen. At this stage of the follow up, a good rapport had been established and the marital interview was acceptable to both sets of parents.

Divorce and Separation

Two couples who had a mongol baby separated permanently before the
marital interview took place. Both marriages had come to the point of
irretrievable breakdown before the index child reached the age of six
months. The first couple were both very young, the mother was aged
twenty-three and the father twenty-one at the birth of the mongol baby.
They already had a healthy son who was thirteen months older than his
mongol brother. At the time of the birth of their second child, the couple
were living in an unsatisfactory furnished cottage while the husband
was working long hours hoping to save enough money for a deposit on a
house. Despite their difficulties with housing and their grief over the
abnormality of their second baby, the marriage had not appeared to be
in danger and the father was severely shocked by the sudden departure
of his wife with another man five months after the birth of the mongol.
The mother maintained very little contact after she had left and only
visited the children once, shortly after her departure. The family were
only enrolled in the study after the mother had deserted, all follow up
interviews have been with the father and, on occasions, also with the
paternal grandmother to whom the family went after the break up.

The second couple had already experienced considerable problems in
their marriage before the birth of the mongol baby. They had previously
considered separation and abortion (see Chapter 3). When they were
finally told of the definite diagnosis six weeks after the birth, the father
refused to have anything more to do with the baby. After a month of
great tension, the mother left the matrimonial home to live with her own
mother. This woman was first seen during the month after she first
heard of the diagnosis and before she left home. At that time there was
no hint of the impending break up. Although after she left home the
father still refused to see the child, the parents kept in touch and went
out together weekly. Both parents co-operated fully with this study and
were both interviewed after the break-up of the marriage. When the
child was two, the mother went ot live in the North of England to be
near her relatives but the mongol boy became ill shortly after the move
and died, after a three week illness, of leukaemia.

The first couple were divorced with a decree absolute being granted
shortly before the mongol baby's third birthday. The second couple
have never taken any steps towards a divorce. The wife remained on
close and affectionate terms with her parents-in-law and on friendly
terms with the husband, although by the end of the study she had no
plans of returning to him.

A temporary separation between husband and wife occurred in the
mongol group of parents, when the wife lived for three months with her

mother before the husband could accept that the mongol baby, his second son, was coming home. Like the couple who eventually were divorced, this pair were in the early twenties.

There were two couples in the mongol group whose baby died and who did not complete the full series of interviews, dropping out before the fourth interview containing the questions to elicit marital data. Data from interviews that had taken place showed no evidence of marital disturbance in one family but considerable evidence of severe tension and hostility between the other couple.

No marriage has broken down in the control group and there have been no temporary separations.

Overall Ratings of the Marriage

Twenty-six families with a mongol baby and all thirty families with a normal control baby completed the full series of interviews. The schedules of the interviews can be found elsewhere (Gath, 1974). All but three interviews had been recorded on tape and had been coded and rated by an independent rater.

The marital relationship was rated overall as follows:

1. mutual concern and affection (good);
2. and 3. generally the same as 1 but with either tensions, quarrels, nagging or loss of mutual concern (moderate);
4. and 5. frequent episodes of open disruption (poor);
6. open antagonism, constant nagging or complete absence of affection (poor).

Six marriages in the mongol group were given ratings of 4 to 6 and were therefore classified as poor. None of the control marriages had ratings of 4 or more. This difference is significant at the 0·05 level (Table 15).

Some estimate can be made of the four marriages in the mongol group for whom no fourth interview was completed. The two complete break-

Table 15

Overall ratings of marital relationships
in the marital interview

Parents	Good	Moderate	Poor	TOTAL
Mongol	14	6	6	26
Control	16	10	0	26
TOTAL	30	16	6	52

$$X^2 = 7·133, \text{d.f.} = 2, p < 0·05$$

Table 16

Overall rating of marital relationship.
All cases

Parents	Good	Moderate	Poor	TOTAL
Mongol	15	6	9	30
Control	19	11	0	30
TOTAL	34	17	9	60

$$X^2 = 10 \cdot 99, \text{d.f.} = 2, p < 0 \cdot 01$$

downs of the marriage are given the rating of 6. Of the two cases where the death of the baby occurred before the fourth interview, one couple, in whose early interviews there was clear-cut evidence of severe tension, hostility and antagonism, can be given a rating of 4, probably an underestimate. The other family who had shown no evidence of tension or hostility in the early interviews and there were positive signs of warmth and empathy, was given the rating of 1. The controls matching these four cases had completed all the interviews. A comparison of the overall ratings of the marital relationship in the total sample of thirty families who had a mongol baby and of thirty matched families who had a normal baby can be seen in Table 16, showing a more marked difference between the two groups.

Detailed Comparison of Marital Relationships

Since four of the marriages in the mongol group can be given only an overall rating, detailed comparison has to be limited to the twenty-six couples for whom the fourth interview was used, coded and rated and to the control couples with whom they were matched.

Sexual dissatisfaction was more common among the parents of mongols than amongst the parents of the control children. More than three times as many parents of the mongol children expressed severe or moderate dissatisfaction with their sexual relationship as did the parents of the normal controls, but since the total numbers are small, the difference is not marked between the groups (Table 17).

Sexual problems including loss of libido were particularly a source of distress to the younger fathers who were in their twenties when their wives gave birth to a mongol. None of these young men had fathered a normal baby before the birth of the mongol. One young man expressed his thoughts on the subject clearly. He said that he had always believed that the one thing anyone could do was to have what he called "an ordinary child". His failure to do what he regarded as a minimal

Table 17

Ratings in the marital interview of sexual dissatisfaction

	None	Mild	Moderate or severe	TOTAL
Mongol	12	7	7	26
Control	16	8	2	26
TOTAL	28	15	9	52

$X^2 = 3 \cdot 428$, d.f. $= 2$, n.s.

achievement made him doubt himself in all other aspects. For six months after the birth of his daughter he suffered loss of libido and was then treated by his general practitioner who gave the father psychotherapy.

Another couple both felt deep disenchantment with sexual activity after the birth of their first child, a mongol. Despite sexual intercourse being irregular and infrequent the wife became pregnant. The birth of a second child who was normal and healthy was a reassurance, and by the end of the period this couple had begun to enjoy their sexual relationship as much as they had before the birth of the mongol child.

One mother of a mongol child had never found satisfaction in her physical relationship with her husband and matters did not improve after the birth of the index baby who was their third child.

Two mothers of the control children, one a first child and the other who had two previous children, had secondary frigidity following the birth.

Mild dissatisfaction with sexual relationships was as common amongst parents of healthy babies as amongst parents of mongol babies (Table 17).

There were slightly more marriages in the mongol group where there were high scores along other dimensions such as tension, hostility, criticism and general dissatisfaction than there were in the control group. These differences, although all in the same direction, did not reach significant levels (Tables 18–21).

Positive measures of marriage relationships are as important as negative measures. Although there were significantly more marriages in the mongol group that had broken or were rated as poor (Table 16), there was no large difference in the numbers of marriages rated as good. Fifteen marriages in the mongol group, half the total, were rated as good, meaning that the relationship was characterized by mutual concern and affection with negligible tension and hostility detected at interview.

Table 18
Ratings of tension in the marital interview

Parents	Low	Moderate	High	TOTAL
Mongol	10	7	9	26
Control	9	11	6	26
TOTAL	19	18	15	52

$X^2 = 1 \cdot 541$, d.f. $= 2$, n.s.

Table 19
Ratings of hostility in the marital interview

Parents	Low	Moderate	High	TOTAL
Mongol	16	6	4	26
Control	20	5	1	26
TOTAL	36	11	5	52

$X^2 = 2 \cdot 334$, d.f. $= 2$, n.s.

Table 20
Level of criticism[a] in marital interview

Parents	None	Moderate	High	TOTAL
Mongol	7	14	5	26
Control	5	20	1	26
TOTAL	12	34	6	52

$X^2 = 4 \cdot 06$, d.f. $= 2$, n.s.

[a] The number of critical remarks were counted and in making the overall rating of criticism mildness or severity of the criticism expressed was taken into account

Table 21
Ratings of general dissatisfaction (excluding sexual) in marital interview

Parents	Low	Moderate	High	TOTAL
Mongol	15	5	6	26
Control	19	5	2	26
TOTAL	34	10	8	52

$X^2 = 2 \cdot 47$, d.f. $= 2$, n.s.

Table 22

Ratings of demonstration of warmth in marital interview

Parents	Little or none	Moderate	High	TOTAL
Mongol	8	7	11	26
Control	8	15	3	26
TOTAL	16	22	14	52

$X^2 = 7.46$, d.f. $= 2$, $p < 0.05$

Significantly more parents of mongols showed demonstration of warmth to one another in the interview as did parents of control babies. Eleven (42%) of the mongol parents showed much warmth compared with three (11.5%) of the parents of controls (Table 22). The same number, eight (30.5%) in each group showed little or no evidence of warmth at interview.

Again, on the positive side, nine healthy babies have been born to couples following the birth of a mongol baby, as many as were born in the control group following a normal baby.

Enjoyment of Children and Maternal Competence

During the same interview as that in which the marital measures were taken, the mothers were asked how much enjoyment they got from their children, including the index child. The majority of the mothers in both groups said they got a great deal of enjoyment out of all their children, but the proportion who said this was somewhat greater in the control group (88%) than in the mongol group (78%). Only one mother said that she had little or no enjoyment in her children. This woman had a strained relationship with her husband and with her two older children who were rebellious and more strongly identified with their English father and their schoolmates than they were with their somewhat tempestuous Italian mother. The mongol baby in this family was amongst the most severely retarded. He was unable to sit until he was eighteen months and was relatively unresponsive in the first year.

The mothers were also asked how they felt that they managed to cope with their children as compared with other mothers. Most mothers in both groups thought that they had some difficulties coping with their children, but that these difficulties were neither more severe nor more numerous than those of other mothers. Certainly there is nothing to suggest that the mothers of the mongols saw themselves as any less competent than did the mothers of the normal babies. Nearly the same number of control mothers (eight or 30·5%) thought that they had more difficulty in coping than most mothers as did the mothers of mongols (nine or 34·5%).

The mothers were also asked if they had difficulty getting through their housework and, if so, if they had more problems than other women in this respect. More control mothers (sixteen or 61%) had no difficulty with housework than did the mongol mothers (nine or 34·5%). Although the mothers of mongols saw themselves as less competent in running the house, the difference is not a large one between the groups. The rating was based entirely on the mother's own perception of how she got through her housework compared with other women she knew. Many of the houses visited in both groups were beautifully kept to a high standard of tidiness and cleanliness. Others were kept in a perfectly acceptable condition but to less perfectionist standards and were more relaxing places, particularly for active children to live in. The mother's views of her ability to cope with housework were related to her ideas of how a home should be run. However, in some cases, the mother's perceived competence at housework seemed at variance with the situation as seen in the home. One mother of a mongol worried as her house was not quite as meticulously tidy as it had been before her daughter began to leave toys around the floor. One control mother whose house was filthy, filled with dirty washing and rotting food, was able to sit amidst such disorder and confidently assert that she had no difficulty whatsoever getting through her work.

Housework was not seen as a very satisfying occupation by the majority of the mothers. Mothers with mongol babies did not differ markedly from mothers of control babies in this respect. Very similar numbers in each group, eight mothers of mongols and seven mothers of controls, said that they were able to derive no satisfaction in performing household duties.

It would seem likely from the data given from this study that the advent of the mongol baby was not as likely to mar a good marriage as to turn a moderate or somewhat shaky marriage into a poor one. The unhappily married were most often those who had experienced considerable conflict as shown by hiding the new born mongol away or wanting to leave it in hospital or considering leaving the neighbourhood when they were first told of the news of the handicap. Although many parents are probably brought closer to one another by their shared tragedy, to other more vulnerable relationships the birth of an abnormal baby can be catastrophic.

7 Brothers and Sisters

The possible ill effect on other children in the family is one of the principal reasons for requesting institutional care for a mentally handicapped child in early childhood. In the course of making a survey of mongol children at home and in institutions in the Oxford area, the following extract was found in the notes of a child aged ten at the time of the survey, who had been in a subnormality hospital from an early age.

> The parents have made application for their daughter to be admitted to a hospital for mental defectives on the grounds that they wish to have more children and feel it would be unwise to do so until —— is removed from the home.

The child was described as a contented baby of sixteen months and she was able to sit and to crawl, but was not yet walking. She was in good general health and had no disabilities other than the obvious facial stigmata of mongolism.

The possible effect on other children is also a potent argument put forward by relatives when one parent is seen as unreasonably insistent on keeping an apparently hopeless baby. It is also the reason why some parents decide to change their aspirations and limit the size of their family, although in general the birth of a mongol baby does not appear to deter relatives significantly from having children (Fraser and Latour, 1968). Many parents, who would be willing to accept their own child for good or ill, are less willing to accept responsibility on behalf of their other children who will have to share the burden at first but may have to carry it alone after the death of the parents.

Advice to consider the interests of the other children in the family is given frequently to parents (Ashley Miller, 1971; Wilks and Wilks 1974) but the situation is not one with a clear choice between home care with definite risks to the other children and institutional care with protection of the normal children from the ill-effects of having a handicapped sib-

ling. Evidence from studies of the brothers and sisters of mentally handicapped children is conflicting.

Holt (1957) concluded that sixty-five (15%) of the four hundred and
thirty siblings were adversely affected by the presence of a mentally
handicapped child in the home. Twenty-four siblings were afraid of
physical attack, eighteen resented the attention given to the handicapped
child, nine had to "help unduly" and six felt ashamed and were teased
by their peers because of the stigma of mental handicap. Schonell and
Watts (1957) also reported that the brothers and sisters in their series
were unable to enjoy normal family outings and holidays. The Wilks
family, referred to above, found that their normal sons could only enjoy
playing with models or trains or reading with their mother if there was
someone else on hand to distract their mongol brother. Other families find
that such "normal" activities as shopping, hair cutting and changing
library books, become so unpleasant a hazard that they are dropped
as far as possible when the handicapped child is at home (Hannam,
1975). Since there are no comparisons made with a control group in
these accounts, caution is necessary in drawing conclusions from these
findings, which need to be interpreted with consideration of how families of similar size, structure and socio-economic status function.

Although the welfare of the siblings may be a common reason for
sending a child away from home, there does not appear to be any substantial evidence that brothers and sisters of children in institutions are
better adjusted than brothers and sisters of similarly afflicted children at
home. Caldwell and Guze (1960) could find no significant differences in
the emotional adjustment of two such groups of siblings. Along with
Graliker et al. (1962), they found that other children in the family tend
to echo their parents' decisions, so that those whose parents had opted
for home care will argue in favour of that, and those whose parents had
decided to send the retarded child away from home will defend that
course of action; a similar reaction to that of children in certain strata of
British society whose parents believe in boarding school education and
those whose parents favour day schools. Only when the parents are not
in agreement with each other do the children have doubts.

The retarded children who live away from home were likely to have
an air of mystery about them and this was not always beneficial to those
left behind in the family home. Doubts about themselves as well as fears
about the retarded child have been sufficiently common and severe
enough for special therapeutic groups for the siblings of children in
institutions to be set up in the United States (Kaplan, 1969). Hannam
(1975) too draws attention to the potentially frightening effect on normal brothers and sisters of putting a retarded child in an institution, and

he also produces samples of sibling behaviour to illustrate the positive side of the relationship between a normal child and his mentally handicapped sibling.

As the mentally handicapped child grows older, his development diverges further from that of the normal child and he requires more care and attention than other children of his age. The majority of brothers and sisters do not resent this extra care. Of the siblings of the mongols in the series described by Barsch (1968), 8% were said to have positive attitudes towards the retarded child. In the siblings survey of one-hundred-and-four families from the same area as the families in this study (Gath, 1973, 1974), many parents pointed out the strong bonds of affection that existed between the normal and retarded children. The mongols from the families who took part in this survey were aged between two and twenty-five, with an average age of eight. Most of the mongols were attending special schools, formerly known as training centres.

Having a mentally handicapped brother or sister at home may well affect boys and girls differently and this is what was found in the one-hundred-and-seventy-four siblings from the families in the Oxford region. The siblings of mongols were all compared with the next child on the school list by means of behavioural rating scales to be completed by parents and teachers. These rating scales had been used previously in studies of children on the Isle of Wight (Rutter *et al.*, 1970) and of London children (Rutter *et al.*, 1974) and were known to be of high reliability and validity. On these scales the brothers of the mongol children were no more disturbed than were other boys in their class, but the sisters were much more likely to have emotional or behavioural problems. These difficulties were usually of an antisocial nature and were most evident at school.

The differences in the reactions of brothers and sisters to a mentally handicapped child in the home may be explained by a difference in roles that boys and girls play at home (Gath, 1974). It was found that disturbed girls from families with a mongol child were more likely to be one of six or more children and to have fathers in unskilled employment. Grammar school girls escaped the ill-effects but the advantages of selective schools may be only a reflection of the social class effect in this sample.

Family Structure

The ordinal position of the mongol babies in the prospective study is shown in Table 23. Nineteen families (63%) had already one or more children at the time of the birth of the mongol. Those brothers and

Table 23

Ordinal position of the mongol babies and their controls

	First born	2nd child	3rd child	4th or later	TOTAL
Mongols	11	7	10	2^a	30
Controls	11	7	10	2^b	30
TOTALS	22	14	20	4	60

a one 10th child b one 6th child

sisters who had already left school and started work were not included in the investigation. There were four such working children in one family where the mongol boy was the tenth child, but five children from that family remained and were included in the study. There were two older children aged twenty-one and eighteen in another family when the third child, the mongol boy, was born. One other family had a working son as well as a schoolgirl daughter when their mongol daughter arrived. Also not included in the investigation of the effect on brothers and sisters were the two children by a previous marriage of a control mother as they only visited their mother's home for short holidays.

There were thirty-two children in the mongol families who were, at the time of the birth of the index child, either going to school or were still too young to attend school. There were thirty-one such children in the control families.

Although the babies themselves were matched for ordinal position, family structure, which would include the spacing of the children as well as the total number and the proportion and distribution of the sexes, was too complex to match with the other variables of social class and neighbourhood. Sibling to sibling matching has not been possible in these families.

Some families, nevertheless, are well matched. One such pair of families each had three girls born within three years, the fathers were in jobs of comparable socio-economic status and the type of neighbourhood was similar. Two other families were very similar at the start of the study, as it was the second marriage for both husbands, both of whom had children by a first marriage, and a first marriage for the wives. The least satisfactory match was that of a pair of families where the mongol child was the tenth in a family who came from rural stock and who has lived in the same village for several generations. No other British born family with anywhere near that number of children had another baby in 1971 in the United Oxford Hospitals. The nearest match was a family whose last baby was their sixth and who also came from an old country family who had also been in their particular village for several generations. However, in this family, two children had died in infancy and there were now only three surviving siblings.

Early Development of the Siblings

Twenty-four of the siblings of the mongol babies had been born by normal delivery, but only fourteen of the control children had a normal delivery. There were three births by Caesarean section in each group, one breech delivery in the control group but four forceps deliveries in the mongol group as opposed to eleven forceps deliveries for control siblings. Four control siblings and one mongol sibling had been unwell in the neonatal period. One sister of a mongol baby had breathing difficulties throughout the neonatal period and in later infancy, during which she had been admitted to hospital three times with chest infections. One control sibling had mild neonatal jaundice, one had feeding difficulties, a third had an operation for pyloric stenosis at two weeks of age and the fourth had an operation for hernia when twelve days old.

All the children in both groups of siblings had achieved the developmental milestones at normal times with the exception of three. These three included one child in each group who was late in talking and one brother of a mongol who was generally backward.

The Health of the Siblings Prior to the Birth of the Index Baby

Six children in each group had been admitted to hospitals after the neonatal period and before the birth of the index baby in this study. Of these six, one in each group had been in hospital in the year immediately preceding the birth of the index baby.

Two boys, one in each group, had three admissions for a similar series of operations (circumcision, tonsillectomy, repair of hernia or undescended testicle). The sister of a mongol baby who had repeated chest infections as a baby, had three admissions for pneumonia, including two in the year immediately before the birth of her mongol brother. Five children, three in the mongol group of families and two in control families, had tonsils or adenoids removed. Brief admissions for observation after head injuries had occurred to two siblings of mongols while three siblings of control babies had been admitted following burns or scalds.

There was a similar pattern of out-patient attendances at hospital as experienced by the children in both sets of families. Most visits involved the casualty department and were the result of minor accidents. There had been two broken arms in each set of families prior to the birth of the index baby.

Frequent visits to the general practitioner had been made by both sets of families concerning the children. During the year before the index birth, twenty-four of the thirty-two mongol siblings (75%) and twenty-two (71%) of the thirty-one control siblings had seen the family doctor on at least one occasion. The most common complaints were sore throats and ear infections for which the parents sought early advice and a prescription for an antibiotic.

The Physical Health of the Brothers and Sisters During the Follow-up Period

During the period of study between the first and last interviews of the series, six children in the mongol group of siblings and seven of the control siblings went to hospital or to a clinic for children. Accidents accounted for two such visits in each group, a broken arm in each group, one sister of a mongol had stitches put in a finger after an accident playing and a brother of a control child broke his nose fighting in the playground.

There were two in-patient admissions in the mongol group of siblings. One child who had her appendix out was the first child in the large family of ten to be admitted to hospital. The other admission was of the little girl who had recurrent chest infections before her mongol brother was born.

Two brothers of mongol babies were referred to clinics at the instigation of their schools. One boy saw the educational psychologist because he was backward in speech and reading and the other boy went to an eye clinic as his teacher thought he was short-sighted.

The hospital and clinic attendance of the children in the mongol group of families was certainly not more frequent than that of the children in the control group. Four siblings of normal babies had short admissions to hospital, three for minor surgery and one to be started on the "buzzer" treatment for enuresis. One control sibling who had chronic constipation was referred to and seen by a paediatric surgeon.

Two of the control children were also seen by their general practitioner for conditions unconnected with the hospital visit. One boy had an allergic reaction and another boy had croup.

Of the children who had no contact with the general practitioner during the follow up period, eight mongol siblings and eight control siblings were said to have had no health problems. Twelve mongol siblings and fourteen control siblings had minor illnesses but did not see a doctor.

Parents differ widely in their policy about taking the child to the surgery. They may be said to have great variation in threshold to the point when their anxiety reaches a level when they seek advice on their child's health. On one home visit to a control family, the three-year-old brother was obviously ill and had a fever. His mother did not call the doctor or take him to the surgery. Another child, this time in the mongol group of families, missed many days from school with repeated attacks of "influenza", sore throats or sickness. He was not taken to see the doctor once in the follow-up period. On the other hand, the older boy in a control family, who was usually a healthy child, was taken to his doctor for an antibiotic as soon as he had a suspicion of a sore throat. There is nothing in this study to suggest that there was any difference in the attitude of the parents in the two sets of families towards the health of their other children. Both sets of families had similar experiences with children's illnesses and minor accidents both before and during the period of study. The parents who had a mongol baby did not become more or less anxious about the health of their other children.

Behaviour and Emotional Symptoms of Siblings up to the Birth of the Index Baby

Parents' Ratings
After the first interview the parents completed the parent behavioural scales A_2 devised by Rutter *et al.*, 1970, on all children who were already going to school. These scales were completed and scored for seventeen siblings of mongol babies and sixteen siblings of control babies. Two siblings in the mongol group had scores of thirteen or more on their scales and four siblings in the control group also had scales on or above that cut-off point. The scales refer to symptoms present in the previous twelve months.

Teacher Ratings
The head teachers of the schools attended by the siblings in both groups were written to as soon as possible after the initial interview with the parents. All the parents who took part in the study agreed to allow the schools to be contacted. One father made the condition that on no account should his children be asked questions by a teacher about the mongol child and that the research should be conducted so that no child should be made to feel "singled out" or conspicuous. This condition was made general and was strictly adhered to throughout the period of study. The head teacher at each school was asked if "the teacher who knows this child best" would complete the Rutter B_2 scales. The scales were returned and scored for thirteen siblings of mongol babies and for twelve siblings of normal babies. One sibling of a normal child had just

changed schools and two other children in this group were enrolled late in the study with the consequence that teachers in their schools would have to rate them twice in a short period of time. The head teacher refused to complete reports on two of the control siblings and there were two children who were enrolled late as in the mongol group.

In each group, there were two children who had scores of nine or more on the B_2 scales completed by their teachers (Rutter, 1967).

Children with Behavioural Problems Before the Birth of the Index Baby

The children with deviant scores on the parent or teacher rating scales are listed in Table 24.

Since both parents and teachers had rated one sister of a mongol as

Table 24

Brothers and sisters with problem behaviour at
time of birth of index baby

Code	A score TOTAL	N^b	A^c	B score TOTAL	N^b	A^c	Parents' assessment of problems[a]	Details
M 9 i	16	5	0	14	2	2	2	Poor relationship with father, hostility over index pregnancy
M 18 i	14	2	3	5	–	–	2	Rebellious
M 18 ii	11	–	–	10	2	0	2	Immature, poor speech and reading
C 8 i	13	5	1	7	–	–	2	Adopted, insecure and immature
C 9 ii	8	–	–	9	0	4	1	Enuretic, not getting on with teacher
C 12 i	14	1	2	0	–	–	1	Healthy, adventurous child in cramped flat
C 15 ii	22	5	4	school refused			2	Poor speech impaired hearing
C 18 i	10	–	–	13	5	0	1	Deprived neighbourhood
C 28 i	13	2	2	late enrolled			2	Anxious mother

[a] Parents' assessment: 0 No problems
1 Some problems, but no more than others
2 More problems than other children
3 Problems requiring treatment
[b] N = Neurotic subscore
[c] A = Antisocial subscore

deviant with scores on or above the cut-off points of thirteen on the A_2 scale and of nine on the B_2 scale, the total number of siblings rated as deviant were three for the mongol group and six for the control group.

No parent thought that their child had any problem requiring treatment. The mothers of the three deviant mongol siblings and of three of the deviant control siblings did, however, believe that their children had more problems than other children. The mothers of the other three deviant control siblings did not think that those children had any more problems than other people's children.

The mother of one child in the control group was also concerned about him even though his scores on both scales were less than the cut-off points. This child had been conceived premaritally and had been placed with a baby minder during the day while his mother worked, until he was eighteen months old. She said of him, "I worry all the time" and she was particularly aware of the contrast between his start in life and that of the index child who was a planned baby born when her parents were secure both emotionally and financially.

The controls had been chosen so that maternal parity was controlled. One family with infertility in the early years of marriage had adopted a child. After the adoption, their own daughter had been born and, four years later, the index child. The girl in this family was a confident and mature child who could do more for herself than could her adopted brother who was nearly two years older. Both parents tried very hard to make the adopted child feel valued and they were at least as devoted to him as they were to the other two children in the family.

Initial rating scores were not completed for the children in the families who had not reached the age of five. The mothers of four of the mongol group of pre-school siblings and of one of the control children had problems in management of their small children. Two sisters were both very timid, inclined to cling to their mother and difficult to get to bed at night. The problems were present at the time of the birth of their mongol sister, but both parents had said that the difficulties had been present for at least a year before the mongol was born. Another girl who had been to hospital with pneumonia twice in the year before the birth of her mongol brother was also very timid. At the time of the first interview this child was overshadowed by her more outgoing elder brother who got on better with his mother. One couple with a mongol baby had much disagreement about the upbringing of the elder son, who was very overprotected, particularly by the father, and was a very immature child who, at the age of four, had had virtually no experience of playing with children of his own age. The disagreements continued when the mongol boy was born but both parents confirmed that the difficulties had been going on for more than two years before. Only one control mother said she had problems with a pre-school child at the time of the interview and this was a young woman who felt she had no control over her first child whose upbringing had been taken over by the paternal grandparents with whom they lived.

Parent/child relationships, as measured by whether the mother wanted the child to be different, whether the child got on its mother's nerves and to which parent the child went if both were present, did not appear to differ between the two groups. Within the groups there was variation such as shown by fathers being the preferred parent of young girls of seven and under but losing this favoured position in the relationship with the older girls, particularly teenagers.

Attitude of Parents to Siblings

Families varied widely in what they expected of their children, in what they would allow their children to do and what they would forbid their children to do. They also varied in how much the parents did with their children. Inter-group comparisons are of little value when there is so much variation between individual families in the groups. The brothers and sisters themselves are therefore used as their own controls and the end of study ratings of these variables are compared with their initial ratings related to each particular child. Table 25 shows the comparison of the parents' expectations and prohibitions of the siblings two years after the birth of the index child as compared with the initial interview. The majority of the parents showed no change in their attitude as

Table 25

Parental expectations and prohibitions of siblings
two years after the birth of the index baby,
as compared with the initial interview

	Siblings of mongol babies	Siblings of control babies
Expectations		
More expected	4	6
Less expected	0	2
No change	15	15
TOTAL	19	23
Prohibitions		
Less prohibited	6	7
More prohibited	1	3
No change	12	13
TOTAL	19	23

measured by the scores on the prohibition part of the interview or on the expectation questions. There is no evidence to suggest that the parents of the mongol children became more restrictive or more demanding of their other children during the period of study than did the parents of normal babies. The scores for expectations and prohibitions are based on a series of questions which are simple and concrete, for example, in the expectation list, the parent is asked if the child cleans his own shoes, "regularly", "sometimes, not regularly" or "never" and similarly under prohibitions the parent is asked if the child "is allowed to leave the house to play or call for his friends without telling you (the parent) where he is going" with the possible answers of "yes, allowed", "sometimes allowed or by one parent only" or "not allowed". The questions were designed by Rutter and Brown (1966) and have been used in previous studies of children on the Isle of Wight and in Camberwell.

The Interaction of the Parents with the Siblings

Parents were asked at the beginning and at the end of the study what they did with their children in the preceding week. A precise description of the activities and the time taken was obtained. The scores were compared for each child and the results are shown in Table 26.

There was little change in the amount of activity shared with the fathers for the majority of siblings in both groups. Slightly more fathers had less to do with their children in the control group at the end of the study but the differences are minimal.

Table 26

Parental interaction with siblings two years after birth of index baby as compared with the initial interview

	Siblings of mongol babies	Siblings of control babies
Interaction with mother		
More	0	3
Less	3	14
No change	16	6
TOTAL	19	23
Interaction with father		
More	1	4
Less	3	5
No change	15	14
TOTAL	19	23

The situation was different for the joint activities with the mothers. Mothers of normal babies were more likely to spend less time with their other children than were the mongol group of mothers who were more likely not to have changed the amount of time given to the other children. The difference between the two groups of mothers was marked in this respect ($X^2 = 7.4$, d.f. $= 1$, p <0.01).

Teacher Ratings of the Siblings at the End of the Period of Study

Teachers completed the Rutter B_2 forms on eighteen siblings of mongol babies and on twenty siblings of control babies. One sister of a mongol had recently moved and changed schools but the new set of teachers did not complete the scale as they felt that they had not known the child long enough. Three children from the families with a normal baby had started school for the first time and they also had not been there long enough for the teachers to get to know them adequately.

Five of the mongol group of siblings and four of the control group of siblings were rated as deviant by the teachers at the end of the study with a score on the B_2 scale of nine or more.

Eleven children from the families with a mongol family and twelve from the control families had school rating scales completed both at the start and at the end of the study. There was no significant difference in the changes in the scores between the two groups. The children were on average two years older at the second rating and none were rated by the same teacher twice.

There is, therefore, no indication that the advent of a baby known to be a mongol has an effect upon the behaviour of the other children in the family as they are observed in school by their teachers.

Parents' Rating of the Siblings at the End of the Study

The A_2 forms were not used again after the initial assessment. Over the series of interviews, an informal and friendly relationship had been built up with each family. The mothers were asked about their children's behaviour and emotional problems in the last interview. The same ground was covered as for the A_2 forms. Symptoms were given a score of one if present but mild or infrequent, and a score of two if frequent or severe. All questions about peer relationships and particularly with sibling relationships were dealt with separately.

Thirteen of the brothers or sisters of mongols had scores of less than five on the interview with the parents as compared with fourteen of the control children. Two children in each group had scores of ten or more. Intermediate scores of five to nine were obtained for four mongol siblings and seven control children. There is no significant difference between the two groups of children according to these scores based on an interview with the mother at the end of the follow-up period.

Parents' Ratings of Pre-school Children

A questionnaire developed by Richman and Graham (1971) was used for the pre-school siblings of three and four years old. Scores were obtained on eight small siblings of the mongol babies and on seven small siblings of the control babies. The cut-off point on this questionnaire is eleven. Only two children scored eleven or more but both of them were from families with a normal baby.

This group of children were present during many of the interviews and it was therefore possible to observe them more than the children who went to school. Four children were seen to present particular problems of management in the mongol group. One such child was a lively, attractive girl who was very demanding of her mother's attention during interviews and was also seen to be overtly jealous of the mongol baby. Another sister was a very shy, timid girl who was very dependent on her mother, but less so than her elder sister who started school just before the end of the study. As mentioned before, however, these girls had difficulties with bed-time and timidity for at least a year before the birth of the mongol baby. The next child in this group was a healthy but very active girl who was very demanding of both parents after the birth of her mongol baby sister. The fourth sibling of a mongol in the pre-school age range to show evidence of problems was the girl who had had recurrent chest infections. However, as the study period was ending her physical health improved and she was beginning to show that, although temperamentally very different from her over-powering elder brother, she was far from dull.

Six of the small siblings of the mongol babies were at a play-group regularly or went to a nursery class while three of the pre-school children in the control group of siblings were at play-group or nursery. No children attended for a full day at a nursery.

Three of the pre-school children in the families with normal babies were seen to have some problems whilst observed during the home interviews. One boy was healthy but a very quiet and timid child. He was often miserable and his play group leader considered him to be a misfit. His mother was comforted when she heard that her husband, a self-confident and successful young man, had been very similar to his son when he was three years old. One mother in the control group of families was struggling to cope with four children under four under the critical eye of her mother-in-law and she found her second child, a boy not quite three at the end of the study, to be completely out of her control. The third pre-school child who obviously had problems was a sad and listless child who was inadequately dressed and cared for. His poor speech could be explained by the general deprivation.

Attitude of the Siblings to the Index Child

Two of the siblings of the mongol babies and one of the siblings of the normal babies were described by their mothers as being hostile to, or jealous of, the baby. These numbers do not include the smaller siblings below the age of five, several of whom were inclined to be jealous. Most of the children (85% in both groups) were said to be very attached to the new baby.

Breaking the News of the Handicap to the Other Children in the Family

Few parents told their other children the news of the handicap until they themselves had had time to digest it. The delay varied from a couple of weeks to several months. Most parents told the other children before they could see anything wrong for themselves. The parents believed that the children should hear about the baby's handicap before there was any risk of hearing about it from an outsider who might not be sympathetic. The family with nine other children were told in two stages by the parents who spoke to the oldest four first about the baby and then the younger five were told a year after that, when some delay in walking was evident. One grandmother undertook to explain to a child that his brother was a "sort of Peter Pan". None of the children told by their parents had noticed anything different about the baby and many of them reacted by protesting that they saw nothing wrong. Three children showed signs of definite distress but their attitude to the mongol child itself remained as had been before. Parents who had dreaded "telling the others" talked of their relief at hearing the older child go into the baby's room next morning and "playing and chatting just as before". Most of the children who were told were said by the parents to have shown no sort of reaction to the news.

At the time the period of study was over, three families had not told their other children that there was anything the matter with the baby. In one family the girls were only two- and three-years-old when the mongol baby was born. Their mother thought them too young to understand then and she was of the same opinion two years later. A second mother had not told her two older children aged seven and five, her mother whom she saw each week, or her neighbours who did not even see the child until he was more than eighteen-months-old. The third mother said of her two sons four and six years older than the mongol "they never asked and I have never said anything".

One boy is known to be a translocation carrier. He was told of his sister's handicap when she was three months old. He and his sister have both had blood taken for chromosomal analysis, but the sister's cells were normal. His parents believed that, at twelve years of age, he was too young to understand the implications of being a carrier. They plan to tell him when he is older, but they were worried about this delicate task.

The Presence of Psychiatric Disorder in the Siblings of the Prospective Study Babies

All the children described or referred to in this chapter were seen on at least one occasion. Of the children, only two were judged to have a behavioural or emotional disorder "sufficiently severe and sufficiently prolonged to cause suffering to the child himself or to others" (Rutter et al., 1970).

"A" was aged eleven when her mongol brother was born and just fourteen at the end of the period of study. She had a very poor relationship with her father, defied her mother by staying out late, was hostile to the mongol child, isolated amongst her peers, miserable and apathetic at school. The diagnosis is that of mixed disturbance of conduct and emotions. This girl had been having problems at school and at home before the mongol was born.

"B" was three-years-old when his mongol brother was born. At the end of the study when he was six, he was very shy, very immature socially, had no friends, had severe separation anxiety going to school and was very dependent even to the extent of still having to be dressed each day. There was disagreement between his parents about his management. He was jealous and very hostile towards the mongol baby. Diagnosis in this case was emotional disorder characteristic of childhood in which the main symptoms involve relationship problems.

Although not suffering from psychiatric disorder as defined, two boys in the control group of pre-school siblings had serious problems.

"C" was a listless, poorly cared for child with speech retardation.
"D" is a problem of management, exacerbated by the difficult home circumstances.

The parents of these children, with the exception of "C", recognized that their chidren had more problems than most but had not sought advice.

There is no evidence in this chapter of any significant difference in the amount of ill health or emotional or behavioural disturbance between the group of siblings of the mongol babies and the group of siblings of normal babies. In the disturbance which was found in a brother or sister of mongols, there is no evidence that the birth of the mongol baby bears any causal relationship to that disturbance. On the contrary, there is evidence that the children had behaviour problems before the birth of the baby in question.

8 The Genetic Implications of the Birth of a Mongol Baby

Many hypotheses concerning the aetiology of mongolism had been put forward since Langdon Down (1866) described his cases and postulated an ethnic theory. These early ideas have been discussed by Penrose and Smith (1966) who cite Jenkins (1933) as an early proponent of the theory that mongolism is related to degeneration of the ovum. Long before, Shuttleworth (1909) had drawn attention to the relationship between a mongol birth and advanced maternal age. The incidence of mongolism was shown to be related to maternal, not paternal, age independently by Jenkins (1933) and Penrose (1933) and to be independent of birth order by Penrose (1933). Chromosomal transmission was suspected for some time before Lejeune et al. (1959) demonstrated 47 chromosomes in mongols in place of the normal 46. It has now been established (Lilienfeld, 1969) that there are three cytological types of mongolism. The first type is caused by non-dysjunction during one of two meiotic divisions occurring in the formation of the ovum so that the child, developing from fertilization of this ovum, has 47 chromosomes, including an extra 21 chromosome thus making a trisomy 21 (Fig. 2). A second type of mongolism has only 46 chromosomes (Polani et al., 1960) but an extra piece of chromosome 21 is attached to another chromosome usually one of the 15 pair. Since chromosomes are also known by letters labelling groups, translocation 15:21 is an interchangeable term with D/G translocation. The translocated chromosome is carried by a phenotypically normal person, with no other abnormalities, and can pass through several generations. The third type of mongolism, in which the patient has some normal and some abnormal cells thus having a total cell structure that is mosaic for normal and trisomy cells, was described by Clark et al., 1961. From a review of a number of surveys, Lilienfeld (1969) estimates that 2 to 3% of mongols are translocation mongols and a further 2% are chromosomal mosaics.

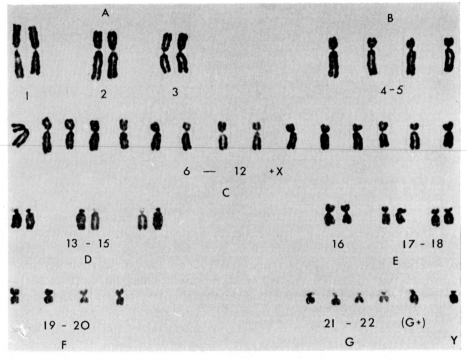

Fig. 2. Karyotype of a child with Down's syndrome, showing trisomy for a G group chromosome.

The Chromosomal Abnormalities in this Group of Mongols

Blood samples had been taken from all the babies in this study when the diagnosis of Down's syndrome was suspected. Twenty-five blood specimens were sent for cell culture and chromosomal analysis to a genetics research department attached to the teaching hospital in the area. Three specimens went to a genetics department to the north, and two others to a third centre in the east.

Twenty-seven babies were found to have the most usual form of chromosomal abnormality found in Down's syndrome, that of 47 chromosomes including trisomy 21. The parents' chromosomes in these cases were all normal in the twenty-four couples and one mother examined (Table 27).

Two babies had chromosomal mosaicism, with some cells with 47 chromosomes and others with the normal 46. One of these children had 93% of her cells with the extra chromosome. She had no features dis-

Table 27

Chromosomal abnormalities found after cell culture

	Maternal age	Infants' chromosomes	Parents' chromosomes
1	31	47–21 trisomy	normal
2	22	47–21 trisomy	normal
3	35	D/G (15:21) translocation	father translocation carrier, mother normal
4	42	47–21 trisomy	normal
5	33	47–21 trisomy	normal
6	35	47–21 trisomy	normal
7	31	47–21 trisomy	normal
8	31	47–21 trisomy	normal
9	44	47–21 trisomy	normal
10	23	47–21 trisomy	normal
11	35	47–21 trisomy	normal
12	41	47–21 trisomy	normal
13	33	47–21 trisomy	normal
14	42	47–21 trisomy	normal
15	42	47–21 trisomy	normal
16	24	47–21 trisomy	normal
17	28	47–21 trisomy	normal
18	27	47–21 trisomy	not examined
19	45	47–21 trisomy	normal
20	24	47–21 trisomy	normal
21	24	47–21 trisomy	normal
22	20	47–21 trisomy	mother normal, father refused
23	43	47–21 trisomy	not examined
24	25	47–21 trisomy	normal
25	25	47–21 trisomy	normal
26	43	47–21 trisomy	normal
27	29	47–21 trisomy	normal
28	22	mosaic 93% 47 cells	normal
29	24	47–21 trisomy	normal
30	21	mosaic 60% 47 cells	normal

tinguishing her from the other children in the group and indeed had more obvious signs of mongolism than some children known to have only trisomy cells. The other mosaic child had 60% of her cells with the extra chromosome. She died too early in the study for any reliable assessment of her development and how it might differ from that of the "ordinary" mongols.

One child had a D/G translocation which was inherited through her father. Her family history is shown in Fig. 3. The brother of this baby

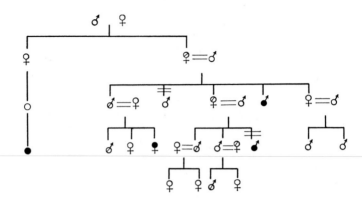

FIG. 3. D/G translocation family.

● = known mongol.

Ø = known carrier.

was also found to be a carrier, but he himself had not yet been told of
this by the end of the study. Much of the family history had been kept a
closely guarded secret as the mother of the translocation mongol did not
know of any mongol in the family until after her own affected daughter
was born. There were two young women in an early stage of pregnancy
in one branch of this family when the translocation was discovered.
Amniocentesis was performed in both cases and ultimately two healthy
babies were born. The other branch of the family, the second paternal
aunt and her immediate relatives, and the paternal grandmother herself
were very resentful of the inquiries into the family history made by the
genetics research workers. They have refused to allow themselves to be
examined and they have been hostile to the family in this study, even to
the extent of severing contact with them. Since the mother of the translocation baby was thirty-five years old at the time of the birth, the discovery of the translocation and the family history was a surprise to the
family themselves and to their doctor.

Four families of children with the trisomy 21 abnormality had another
mongol somewhere in the family. The father of one of the mongols had a
brother with a six-year-old mongol daughter who was well-known to the
study family. Another father had a first cousin with a mongol child and
in this case too the older child was a regular visitor to the family before
their own affected baby was born. The other two families had more
remote histories of mongolism in the family, in one case the half sister of
the maternal grandmother had had a mongol who had died in childhood and a paternal great-aunt in another family had a mongol of
which little was known.

Subsequent Pregnancies During the Period of Study

Nine healthy babies were born to mothers after the birth of the mongols during the period of the study and this is the same as the number of babies born to the mothers who had had the normal babies. One mother in each group was pregnant at the end of the study.

One of the subsequent babies born to mothers of mongols was unplanned, as was one baby born to a control group. The rest of the babies born after the index baby in each group were conceived as a result of a definite wish to have a child. The subsequent child came a little sooner in the mongol families as the mean gap in months between the birth of the index child and the birth of the subsequent baby was twenty-one months for the mongol group and twenty-four months ten days for the control group.

Amniocentesis

Foetal cells can be obtained from the amniotic fluid surrounding the foetus and can be cultured and used for chromosomal analysis. The fluid can be drawn off from the mother through a needle in the abdominal wall once the uterus has reached sufficient size to be accessible, usually about fourteen to sixteen weeks of gestation. The cell culture may take two weeks or even longer to analyse. The method enables chromosomal abnormalities to be diagnosed *in utero* and it has been advocated that the procedure should be available to all women at risk of having a child with such an abnormality (Stein *et al.*, 1973).

Women who have already had a mongol child are at increased risk of another (Berg and Kirman, 1961). Amniocentesis was attempted in three such women. These mothers were aged thirty-one, twenty-seven and twenty-four when the mongol babies were born. A specimen of amniotic fluid was obtained in all three cases but one cell culture failed to grow. The other two women were both told that the child they were expecting was not a mongol and they were also told the sex of the child.

Two other mothers asked for amniocentesis to be done in their subsequent pregnancies after the birth of a mongol baby with trisomy 21. One of these women who was twenty-four at the birth of her mongol son said that her general practitioner did not agree to refer her to the centre twenty miles away where the test could be performed. The second woman had a previous miscarriage, before the birth of the mongol, and was advised by her obstetrician that amniocentesis could increase the chance of her miscarrying again.

Two women knew about the possibility of amniocentesis and that it could be performed if they wished. They both decided against it. As one said "we have managed all right with this one and we will take what comes again". They both knew that the results of the amniocentesis would not be available until about seventeen to eighteen weeks of pregnancy and neither were happy at the thought of a termination at that stage.

The last two women who gave birth to a child after a mongol did not know of the possibility of the test and were not told about it during their pregnancy. When discussing amniocentesis in the comfortable situation of having given birth to a healthy baby, these women had said they were glad that they had not known about the procedure but they both said that they had many worries during the pregnancy.

Pregnancies Ending Before Term

In addition, there were three pregnancies in the mongol group which ended before three months. One woman, who later had a normal boy, had a hydatidiform mole, a degenerative disorder of the chorion occurring in the first half of pregnancy. Another woman amongst the mothers of mongols in this group had a hydatidiform mole before the birth of her mongol baby.

Two women had terminations, including one young woman with marital difficulties and another who was twenty years old when her mongol boy, her second child, was born.

There were no miscarriages and no therapeutic abortions in the control group.

Family Planning

Of the pregnancies coming to term, eight of the nine occurred in women whose mongol child had been their first baby. The ninth woman said

Table 28

Family planning methods two years after
birth of index baby

	Parents	
	mongols	controls
Avoidance of intercourse	3	0
Rhythm method or withdrawal	7	4
Sheath or diaphragm	2	4
Oral contraception	2	7
Intrauterine device	3	2
Vasectomy	4	4
Tubal ligation/hysterectomy	4	4
Pregnant at time	1	1
TOTAL	26	26

that she and her husband had originally decided only to have two children for environmental and other reasons concerned with world population. As the second had been a mongol, they had then decided that they would be wise for the sake of themselves and their other child to have a third, arguing that their entitlement was to have two normal children.

Table 29

Sterilization following mongol birth

	Method	Reason	Completed family size
A. Sterilization of mother			
Mongol families	hysterectomy	menorrhagic/ enough children	3 + mongol who died
	tubal ligation after 2nd birth	first child mongol, hyperemesis twice	2
	tubal ligation after index birth	3rd Caesarean section (diagnosis of mongolism not yet made)	3
	tubal ligation and termination	2nd child mongol	2
Control families	tubal ligation after 2nd birth	maternal age and hypertension	2
	tubal ligation after index birth	3rd Caesarean section	3
	tubal ligation after index birth	maternal hypertension	3
	tubal ligation after 4th birth	enough children	4
B. Sterilization of father			
Mongol families	vasectomy	translocation carrier	3
	vasectomy	2nd child mongol	2
	vasectomy	wife's hypertension 3rd child mongol	3
	vasectomy	3rd child mongol	2 + mongol who died
Control families	vasectomy	enough children, father had four by previous marriage	2 (+4)
	vasectomy	enough children	4
	vasectomy	wife's renal disease	2
	vasectomy	enough children	4

D

Seven of the nine births in the control group were to mothers whose first child was the control in the study.

In eight families in each group, one of the parents was sterilized during the period of study. Four fathers in the mongol group and four in the control group had a vasectomy (Table 28).

Four mothers in each group were sterilized. Two control mothers had a tubal ligation done immediately after the birth of the index baby. One mother in the mongol group also had had a tubal ligation done immediately after the index birth, her third Caesarean section before the diagnosis of mongolism had been made (Table 29).

All four fathers in the control group had their vasectomies done privately. They were satisfied with both their decision and the way in which it was implemented. The vasectomy operation was on the National Health Service for two of the fathers of mongols. One of these men was the translocation carrier and the other man had a poorly paid, irregular job, lived in condemned housing and had a mongol boy, his third child, with severe heart disease. One of the fathers in the mongol group who had a private vasectomy was content with the speedy and efficient way in which it took place but the other couple were confused and somewhat bitter that they had to pay for the operation, particularly as the wife had hypertension, the mongol boy was already hyperkinetic and they were living on a relatively low wage.

Only one mother regretted having made the irreversible decision regarding further children. She was twenty years old when her second child, the mongol, was born and had a healthy boy one year older. A year after the birth of the mongol baby, she had a termination and sterilization. She believed that her chances of having another afflicted child were particularly great because she had been so young at the birth of the mongol boy, who had however a trisomy 21 abnormality and was not a translocation. Her regret about her sterilization was connected with her unhappy marriage and she tended to compensate for her disappointments by being over-protective and over-indulgent to her normal boy.

Surprisingly, the effect of the birth of an abnormal baby was not to make the parents use the most reliable method of contraception (Table 29). Ten (39%) of the parents of mongols were relying on avoidance of intercourse, withdrawal or the rhythm method. More control parents use oral contraception.

The results of the cell culture and chromosomal analysis were explained to parents, usually by the paediatrician or the geneticist himself. The incidence of mongol births is about 1 in 688 live births (Collman and Stoller, 1962) who showed that the incidence varies with the age of the mother so that the risk increases after thirty to a peak incidence around the age of forty, but with the risk continuing to go up, despite the falls in births, as maternal age increases. Approximate, rounded risk figures are given as 1 in 2000 at age of twenty, 1 in 1000 at age thirty, 1 in 150 at forty and 1 in 50 at forty-five. Although having had one mongol with trisomy 21 and normal parental chromosomes increases the chances, a woman of twenty-one with one mongol would still have a much smaller chance of a mongol birth than a woman of forty with no previous history. In this light, the sterilization of a twenty-one year old girl could be regarded as somewhat drastic. On the other hand, some parents are willing to take a larger risk. One woman of forty-four was still hoping to become pregnant again after the birth of her mongol son when the risk quoted to her was a chance of 1 in 20 of another afflicted child. Several multiparous women aged more than thirty-five in the mongol group were not wanting another baby but were relying on unreliable methods of contraception.

Despite the birth of an abnormal baby, the subsequent behaviour of the parents in relation to contraception and reproduction did not differ from that of parents of normal babies. There were the same number of live births in both groups, confirming the finding of Fraser and Latour (1968) that the birth of a mongol child does not deter a family who wish to have more children. Although eight couples decided on sterilization, a reliable but almost invariably irreversible method of contraception, this decision was also taken by the same number of parents who had had a normal child. Although all parents of mongols had access to genetic advice as blood samples had been taken from every child and from all but two couples among the parents, ten couples had made no contact with either their doctor or a clinic in order to obtain advice on family planning and were still using unreliable methods of contraception, if any. Genetic counselling can have little effect unless it is linked with family planning advice.

Genetic Counselling

The speciality of medical genetics has grown rapidly in importance over the past fifteen to twenty years. From a largely research unit, the department in the Region where this study was carried out has now developed into a more clinically orientated specialist department where the emphasis is on advising families who may have cause for anxiety about the outcome of a particular pregnancy or may be concerned about future reproduction after the birth of a defective child.

Genetic counselling consists largely of explaining the facts of their case to a family, describing the risks involved and then allowing the family themselves to make an informed decision. The possibility of prenatal diagnosis through amniocentesis has made the general public more aware of genetic abnormalities and the possible need for advice.

Women who already have given birth to an abnormal child are one group who are referred for genetic advice. First the diagnosis of the abnormality must be made. Some genetic counsellors are themselves paediatricians or specialists in subnormality while others work in close conjunction with a paediatric department offering diagnostic skills and procedures. The condition may be known to be due to environmental trauma, such as infection during pregnancy, and the genetic counsellor may then be able to explain this to the parents and reassure them that in the next pregnancy they will have no more chance than anyone else of having an abnormal child. Inherited conditions may be due to a chromosomal abnormality such as in Down's syndrome, to a single major gene or to multi-factorial inheritance involving interaction of several genetic and environmental factors (Bobrow, 1977). Scrutiny of the family history with construction of a pedigree and calculation of recurrence rates will distinguish single gene effects from the multi-factorial inheritance.

Down's syndrome is the most common of a group of disorders where there is an extra chromosome either free or attached to another chromosome (Ford, 1973).

Diagnosis of Down's syndrome is now almost always confirmed by examination of the baby's blood and demonstration of this extra chromosome. The parents' blood is also examined, particularly if the subject has a translocation, to determine which parent is a carrier. In most cases the blood taken from the parents shows no abnormality. The risk quoted to parents with normal chromosomes themselves is that there is one chance in a hundred of them producing another affected child (Lindenbaum, 1977). The examination of the baby's and parents' blood occurs shortly after clinical diagnosis and the parents may still be unable to take in the facts presented to them. The session with the medical geneticist does give them the opportiunty to discuss the cause of the condition and the implications that it has for their family. The handling of the genetic counselling interview is described by Bobrow (1977) who indicates the need for sensitivity on the part of the counsellor and the awareness of how the facts he may present could affect the relationship between the parents. There are also difficult ethical and moral issues (Fletcher, 1975).

As most women having babies are in their early twenties, the distribution of maternal age of a group of mothers of Down's syndrome children extends over a wide range (Figs 4 and 5). In this study eleven mothers were thirty-five or more. In discussing the prevention of Down's syn-

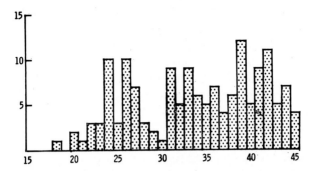

FIG. 4. Maternal age and mongolism: age of mother at birth of mongol baby. 150 cases.

Horizontal axis = age in years.
Vertical axis = number.

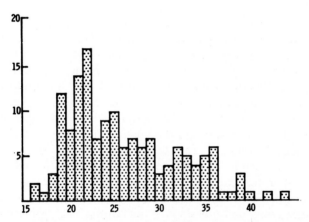

FIG. 5. Maternal age: 150 consecutive deliveries at Churchill Hospital.

Horizontal axis = age in years.
Vertical axis = number.

drome, Alberman (1975) states that an important method of prevention is to encourage mothers to have their babies before the age of thirty when the risk is very low. There have been changes in maternal age distribution in which there has occurred a steady fall in the proportion of babies born to older mothers but there is insufficient evidence to show that there has been a drop in incidence secondary to these changes.

Amniocentesis in which amniotic fluid is drawn off to obtain foetal cells whose chromosomes can be studied is advocated for pregnant women of thirty-five or more. Recent figures from the Department of Medical Genetics at Oxford (Lindenbaum, 1977) show that chromosome exam-

ination from amniocentesis specimens were done for one hundred and
sixty-four mothers of thirty-five or more in the years 1974 to 1976. In this
group, antenatal diagnosis, and therefore prevention, was made of three
Down's syndrome foetuses (trisomy 21), three Edward's syndrome, a
condition incompatible with long life (trisomy 18), and one other with
an extra sex chromosome (XXY). Lindenbaum (1977) calculated that
only 2·8% of women of thirty-five or more were being referred for
amniocentesis. If there was a 100% amniocentesis rate in this age group,
then forty-two Down's syndrome babies would be diagnosed antenatally
and probably prevented in this region. There is therefore a very low rate
of referral for high risk mothers but even 100% screening would only
halve the numbers of affected children born. Forty-one women who had
had a previous mongol child were referred for amniocentesis and no
chromosomal abnormalities were found antenatally in this group between 1974 and 1976.

One reason for the low rate of referral is that amniocentesis cannot
take place until at least fourteen weeks after conception and the results
may not be known for three weeks. Diagnosis is therefore rarely possible
before seventeen to eighteen weeks gestation. Many women have already
felt movements by that time, particularly if they have had a previous
child. Termination of pregnancy at this stage is not the same compara-
tively easy process as it was at six to eight weeks gestation. Amniocentesis, the wait for the result and the possible termination all add up to a
very considerable stress.

Translocation produces a greater risk of another affected child, a risk
quoted as one in ten but it is thought that if the father is the carrier the
risk may not be as great. This situation requires careful explanation to
parents and to the other members of the family. The problems of genetic
counselling are considerable. There is a conflict between parental desire
for another child and the size of the burden as seen by the family. The
role of the counsellor (Bobrow, 1977) is to provide information on which
the parents may then take a decision. In the process of decision making,
the counsellor is not completely neutral, although it is stressed that those
being counselled must take the decision and inevitably bear the brunt of
the consequences. Follow up of the effects of genetic counselling show
some relief of anxiety (Antley and Hartlage, 1976) and some change in
the reproduction intentions of the families with a high risk of recurrence.
However, even those who state they are deterred from further pregnancies may not take any contraception precautions (Leonard et al., 1972).
The decisions made should be related to the primary care team so that
the family doctor can arrange for contraception advice, either in a clinic
or on a domicillary basis.

9 The Social and Medical Support of the Families

The "nuclear" family of parents and children can not be looked at in isolation from the larger unit or "extended" family, consisting of grandparents, uncles, aunts and cousins. The stability of the smaller unit is influenced by relationships between it and its individual members with the larger unit and its individual members, as well as by the bonds and tensions within the immediate family group living in the same home. A new baby becomes the focus of interest for most families and often provides an occasion for a reunion. Where celebration of a birth changes to sadness as the child's abnormality is recognized, the larger family unit cannot avoid being affected by the event and influencing what happens next.

A key figure is the maternal grandmother. Animal studies, notably those of Harlow and Harlow (1969) have shown that adequate experience of being mothered is necessary for an animal to be able to provide maternal care in her turn. The studies of child abuse indicate that human mothers also learn nurturing behaviour in early childhood, as those who later abuse children have more often been abused themselves or to have had little or no experience of a loving relationship with the adult who cared for them (Steele and Pollock, 1974; Sameroff and Chandler, 1974). Separation from their mothers in early childhood was shown by Frommer and O'Shea (1973) to be an important factor in determining how well pregnant women would adapt to the task of caring for their own infants.

A close relationship with the maternal grandmother has been found to be a positive factor in families with a handicapped child. Farber (1959) found that close contact with the wife's mother was associated with greater marital integration in the parents of a retarded child, but close contact with the husband's mother was not. A mother of a child with cystic fibrosis (Burton, 1975) is quoted as describing her own mother as very understanding but her mother-in-law as making it "a thousand times worse" but she qualifies this by saying that her mother-in-law worried so much. Mothers, or mothers-in-law, who wept or worried visibly when visiting the handicapped child and its parents were understandably seen as unhelpful as were also those who dismissed the problem either by denial or by futile reassurances that the child would "outgrow it".

The Grandmother

In the year immediately before the birth of the baby in this study, more mothers who were later to have normal babies had seen their own mothers at least once a week than had the mothers who later gave birth to mongols (Table 30). There was a similar but less marked difference in the contacts between the families and the paternal grandparents. The families did not change their pattern of visiting significantly in the two years following the birth of the baby as two-thirds of the families with a mongol baby and the same proportion of the families with a normal baby visited, or were visited by, the maternal grandparents as frequently or more often than they had done in the years before the birth.

One year after the birth of the baby concerned the mothers were all asked how much support they had had during that year from their own mothers. Half the mothers in each group rated the maternal grandmother as giving much support. The comment: "She is behind me in whatever I do" typified the attitude that these women had towards the maternal grandmother in 50% of both groups of families. Strong, warm but uncritical support of this sort was particularly appreciated by the

Table 30

Social contact with relatives in the year before the birth
of the index baby

	Families of mongols	Families of controls
A. Contact with maternal grandparents		
At least once a week	12	21
Less than weekly	18	9
TOTAL	30	30

$$X^2 = 4\cdot3, \text{d.f.} = 1, p < 0\cdot05$$

	Families of mongols	Families of controls
B. Contact with paternal grandparents		
At least once a week	11	17
Less than weekly	19	13
TOTAL	30	30

$$X^2 = \text{no significant difference}$$

mothers of the mongol babies when they looked back to the first agonizing days after they had learnt of the baby's handicap. When they were
making decisions, they were able to believe that their own mothers
would not try to influence their decision but would support them however they made their choice. This sort of moral support from the maternal grandmother appeared to be more important than proximity of
relatives. One mother had her nearest relatives, her parents and a
brother living nearly two hundred miles away and the families met only
once a year. Yet close emotional contact was maintained by weekly
telephone calls and this mother was one of those most appreciative of her
parents' concern.

Practical support from the maternal grandmother took many forms.
Babysitting enabling the parents to go out together or the mother to
window-shop or have her hair done was a much appreciated service
offered regularly by the supportive grandmothers. Financial help in
terms of gifts of money or, more indirectly, as gifts of clothing for the
children, was another common form of practical help.

In a few cases where the maternal grandparents had died, lived far
away or were on bad terms with their daughter, the paternal grandparents took over the role as supporters of the family. In one such case,
the mother of a mongol boy had been on very bad terms with her own
mother throughout her adolescence and was finally turned out of the
house when she became pregnant at the age of sixteen. This pregnancy
ended in a miscarriage and the young woman remembers her mother
telling her at the time that she would never be able to have a normal
child. When she married when she was twenty, this particular mother
was very dependent on her parents-in-law and very grateful to them for
their practical and affectionate support during the first year after the
birth of her mongol son. However, a year after the birth, a sister-in-law
returned from abroad bringing two more grandchildren into the family.
The mother in this study felt very rejected and became highly suspicious
and resentful of her relatives-in-law. A suggestion that too close a relationship with the paternal grandparents indicates a mother with an
emotionally deprived childhood is supported by this particular case, and
also by the lack of positive correlation found between contact with paternal grandmother and stability of the family with a retarded child (Farber, 1959).

In both cases in which there was a complete breakdown of the marriage
in the year following the birth of the mongol, the grandparents played
a crucial role supporting the parent left to bring up the child alone. In
one of these cases, a young man was left with a normal boy who was not
yet two years old and a mongol boy aged six months. He returned to live

with his widowed mother and his unmarried brother and sister. Although the father firmly insisted on doing most of the parenting work himself, he was only able to do this with the support of the rest of the family. In the other case in which the marriage had failed, the mother returned to the maternal grandmother with whom she shared the care of the mongol boy and was therefore able to have a part-time job and outside interests which helped her during the painful days after the separation from her husband.

More mothers with normal babies had said that they had no help of any significance from their own mothers in the first year after the birth of the baby enrolled in the study. They felt this lack of support but, because the children were healthy and their marriages at least reasonably happy, they were able to cope.

The two other women in the group with mongol babies who had no support from their own mothers had no compensatory sources of help as in one case the paternal grandparents were both dead and, in the other, the hostility of the paternal grandparents, who blamed their daughter-in-law for the break up of their son's first marriage, was much increased by the birth of the handicapped child and the parents' decision to take him home. These two women were pitifully lonely and often depressed with no close friends and, by the end of the study, it was evident that their babies were amongst the most mentally retarded.

The Health Visitor

Two mothers who had warm and affectionate relationships with their own mothers but were rarely able to see them for geographical reasons were glad of the regular, friendly visits of their health visitor. The reliability of the health visitor and her willingness to sit down to share a pot of tea and listen was appreciated more than the advice she had to give. Health visitors are obliged to visit each mother with a new baby once and thereafter regard the baby as their special concern until the time comes for him to go to school. The visits to the home did not continue where the health visitor saw no need for this service and so the frequency of health visitors' home visits was less in the families with a normal baby (Table 31).

The health visitors rarely had had any substantial experience of the problems of families with a mongol child, but some made considerable efforts to learn and to pass information on to the families. It was resented when they merely repeated clichés about the guilt of mothers of handicapped children and were found to have an almost complete ignorance of the practical problems.

More than a third of the mothers of the mongols found the visits of the

Table 31

Frequency of health visitor's visits to the home

Frequency of visits	Mongol families	Controls
At least once a month	8	1
At least once every 3 months	16	8
Less than once every 3 months	6	21
$X^2 = 16\cdot43$, d.f. $= 2$, p $<0\cdot001$		

health visitor to be very helpful but despite the greater efforts made to visit the families of the mongol children, there was not a marked difference in the ratings of the helpfulness of the health visitors between the two groups. More of the mothers of the healthy babies encountered the health visitor at the Infant Welfare Clinics (for normal children). Only two mothers in the control group never went to the clinic as both said that they saw no need to go with a healthy baby who was not the first born. On the other hand, seven mothers of mongol children never went to the clinic but the reason given was different as they all felt in need of help but "could not face all those mothers with their normal babies".

The General Practitioner

The family doctors were asked to see the children with Down's syndrome more often than they were consulted about the control children. This finding is hardly surprising in view of the high incidence of congenital heart disease and other abnormalities. Perhaps a larger difference in the medical attention required could have been expected but some of the parents of the mongols felt it was not so necessary to keep in close touch with their general practitioner when they were regularly attending paediatric out-patients.

The general practitioners were much appreciated by two-thirds of the mothers in the control group who rated them as very helpful in the first year after the birth of the baby. Nearly as many of the mothers of mongols had the same degree of satisfaction with their family doctors to whom they brought more problems than did the mothers in the control group. There were some general practitioners who were outstanding in the quality of care and support they gave to the families with mongol children. One such doctor, with a near relative who was a mongol, ran his own paediatric clinic and spent much time listening to and explaining to the two mothers in this study who were on his list of patients. In contrast, other mothers complained that their general practitioners had no knowledge of babies such as theirs and that they gave the impression that they considered such children as less than human. One woman who attended her doctor's surgery regularly for pills for her "nerves" was deeply distressed that on no occasion was any reference made to her affected son. These women were likely to have become over-sensitive and quick to misinterpret any brusqueness in manner, but their comments indicate a failure in the doctor–patient relationship.

The Paediatrician
Twenty-two of the parents of the mongol children made at least three visits to the paediatric out-patient department of a general hospital. For some parents, these visits required considerable effort, involving travelling some distance and the necessity of the father asking for time off work. It is disappointing for all concerned that nearly half the parents found these visits to be of little use. The reasons they gave most often included these three; first the long time waiting compared with the short time during which the child was actually seen by the doctor; second the lack of continuity, which was particularly applicable to the teaching hospital where registrars and junior lecturers appeared to change rapidly and "to have to spend all our allotted time reading the notes"; and third, the emphasis on the child's physical health, particularly the detection of any heart lesion, rather than on his development as a whole.

The visits to the out-patient department were regarded as most helpful when the child and parents were regularly seen by the consultant paediatrician. In those cases, in which it had been the consultant himself who had broken the news early to the parents and had then followed it up by providing regular appointments with adequate time to examine the child and to allow questions and discussion, there was much more satisfaction with paediatric services.

The Psychiatrist Specializing in Mental Handicap
Only one family was referred to a psychiatrist specializing in mental handicap during the first two years after the birth of a child with Down's syndrome. In the single case, the boy was admitted twice during his second year "to give the mother a rest". The first admission appeared to have the intended effect but the second made this mother more anxious. By that time, she had also visited the local school for mentally handicapped children and she had noticed that the children who lived at home and went daily to school appeared less retarded and less disturbed than the hospital patients. In addition, her own child had reacted to the second admission in much the same way as any child of average intelligence reacts to short term separation from his mother as, on returning

home, he had been more demanding and anxious about possible threats of a repeated separation. Far from giving her a rest, this second admission had produced more problems.

Several other mothers had been told about services available through the hospitals for the mentally handicapped but none of them made any approach or inquired further as they had anxieties about the child being "put away".

One child in the mongol group had bilateral cataract and, despite several operations, was blind. This mother was very concerned about his double handicap. During the first two years, no one, including the general practitioner and the paediatrician, had mentioned to her the existence of a special unit for blind retarded or disturbed children which was in the same hospital board region, although admittedly at the opposite end of it.

The National Society for Mentally Handicapped Children

Eighteen out of the thirty families had joined the Society for Mentally Handicapped Children by the time the children in this study had reached the age of two. This proportion is slightly more than those who joined the society in the group studied by Carr (1975). One parent, at least in six of the families, had attended a meeting of the Society. At this early stage the meetings were not found to be very relevant to the problems being encountered by the families but those who had joined the Society thought that they would derive more practical benefits when their children were older and attending school.

Eleven families were visited by another parent of a mongol child so that in all, fourteen families, less than half the total, had some direct contact with other parents in the same predicament. Out of the fourteen, four found that the contact with another parent or the Society to be very helpful, nine found some help from the contact, but one set of parents thought that their contact with another parent had been actually discouraging.

If the four families whose babies died before the completion of the series of interviews are excluded, there remain twelve families who had no contact with either the Society for Mentally Handicapped Children or with other parents of similar children. Eight couples said that they wanted no contact at all and that they would not have welcomed an approach from either another parent of a mongol child or from a representative of the Society but four couples said that they would have welcomed such an approach.

These findings are very similar to those of Carr (1975). Some parents join groups more readily than others, who are perhaps shyer. The main

E

reasons given for not joining the Society and for not wanting to meet other parents were connected with the parents' expressed fears of becoming too much a part of an ostracized minority group. They wanted to remain part of the normal population for as long as possible.

Religion

Church membership was little more than nominal in most cases, although 60% of the mongol babies and 66% of the control babies had been christened.

Although almost without exception the parents talked of the significance of the birth of an abnormal child in relation to religious beliefs; their religious practice in terms of church attendance changed very little during the two years following the birth of the child. What changes took place were very similar to those found in the control families.

Religion was an important part of life to several parents, particularly to two couples with a mongol baby who said that their religion had been a significant source of strength to them. One woman who had been an active church member all her life said that she felt specially picked out by God to be the mother of a handicapped child. Others with more lukewarm beliefs were likely to see the event of the birth of the malformed child as evidence that God had little regard for them, and an atheist thought that it proved his point that there was no God. Other parents were influenced by the attitude of the local priest. One couple who originally felt shamed by the stigma of a retarded child finally came to accept the child and regard her as accepted by the community when she was chosen to take the part of the Christ Child in the village Nativity Play. Another woman who had remained a devout Catholic throughout her marriage despite her husband's jeers was deeply grieved by her parish priest's seeming indifference to her baby's death.

Social Workers

Although some families had met a social worker in the hospital where the baby was born, there was no continued contact after the child had been taken home.

Two families approached the local authority social services for help. One set of parents were a well educated and articulate couple but both came from aloof and unsupportive families. At first they were ambivalent in their attitude toward the baby, not wanting to keep her and yet anxious to do their best for her. The social worker assigned to them had a sympathetic attitude which made them feel more relaxed and more affectionate toward the mongol baby. A friendly foster-mother was found to care for the child for occasional Sundays and when the parents went on holiday. The social worker's intervention in this family was of considerable benefit.

A less successful appeal for help to the social services was made by the other couple who were less eloquent and had many other problems. The mother in this family had to spend two months in hospital before the birth of her second child. The father's appeals to the Social Services then produced no practical help and he had to give up his job to care for the mongol boy, then aged sixteen months. The parents were both very distressed when after the mother had been discharged with the second child, a healthy boy, a social worker then called to discuss institutional care for the mongol who was then presenting no more problems than any other normal child of his age.

Social Changes During the Period of Study

There were a number of changes in the lives of both groups of families in the two years following the birth of the baby. One third of the fathers in both groups had changed jobs. Four fathers in the mongol group of families had changed their jobs twice or more often as compared with one father in the control group. Similarly, seven families in both groups had moved house but three of the families in the mongol group had moved twice or more as compared with one control family. There is no evidence therefore that the birth of the abnormal child deterred the family in its natural tendency to improve its way of life by moving house or changing the bread-winner's occupation. There is a suggestion, but nothing more, that some families may have become less settled after the birth of the mongol child.

The same number of mothers were working full-time or part-time by the end of the study, six in each group. Two mothers of mongol babies enrolled in the Open University in the second year and both derived much satisfaction from the academic challenge although they had to use considerable skill to arrange their time to fit in with the domestic demands.

Social contacts with the extended family and with friends showed some changes and adjustments after the birth of the baby in both groups. The changes were not more frequent when the baby had Down's syndrome than when the baby was normal.

These findings are similar to those found by Barsch (1968), Hewett (1970) and Carr (1975). Some people are by nature "joiners" and others are more inclined to be "loners". The social supports of the families and the amount they were used depended less on the handicap of the child and more on the customary pattern of social behaviour of the families, as indicated by their way of life before the birth of the affected child. Nevertheless, the most distressed mothers were those who had little or no support from relatives, no compensatory social life and had no regular contact with a social worker, health visitor or doctor. They were always very co-operative with and hospitable to the research worker who had reason to believe that regular home visiting by someone interested in them and their children would be welcomed.

10 The Interaction of the Different Effects on the Family

The most striking difference between the families with a mongol baby and the families with a normal baby is shown in the number of broken or disharmonious marriages in the mongol group. Since there was a similar number of good marriages in the two groups, it seems probable that the arrival of a baby with a congenital malformation sufficiently severe to cause handicap throughout the child's life does not mar a good marriage but has the potential to disrupt the balance of a moderate or more vulnerable marriage.

Effects on the health of the parents are not so clear-cut. There is little evidence as presented in Chapter 5 of a detrimental effect on the physical health of parents as shown in a difference between the number of medical contacts made by the two groups of parents. Psychiatric ill health was more common in the parents of mongols but the difference is not a large one.

Ill health, physical or psychiatric, could be associated with unhappi-

Table 32

Parents' marital relationship and parental illness (both groups of families)

	Good	Moderate	Poor	TOTAL
A. All medical contacts in either parent				
Medical contact	20	13	8	41
No medical contact	14	4	1	19
TOTAL	34	17	9	60
X^2 test for trend $p < 0.05$				
B. Psychiatric illness in either parent				
With psychiatrically ill parent	11	7	3	21
No psychiatrically ill parent	23	10	6	39
TOTAL	34	17	9	60

ness in the marriage. One or other parent in eight out of the nine most unhappy marriages had had some sort of medical contact and, over all, there was a trend for contact with medical agencies to be more common when the parents had severe tension or discord between them (Table 32). This trend is not seen when consultations for psychiatric conditions alone are considered in relation to unhappiness of the marriage.

Marital disharmony and illness

Mothers who have had some medical contact in the follow-up period become more frequent with deteriorating marital relationships. The trend reaches significant proportions only when all mothers in both groups are considered but can be seen to a lesser degree when the mothers in the mongol group are considered alone. On the other hand, ill health in the fathers, also as demonstrated by medical contacts, does not appear as more common in the poor marriages.

Of the ten women who had depression, five had had treatment from their general practitioners and five had been found to be clinically depressed at interview. Only two of the depressed women came from the nine most unhappy marriages and five depressed women had marriages rated as good with no significant evidence of tension, hostility or lack of warmth. Certainly the depressed women were suffering and required treatment of some sort, either psychopharmacological or psychotherapeutic. Yet concentration on the overt mental ill health of the mothers would not avert or appreciably affect the detrimental effects of an abnormal child upon the marriage. Similarly only one psychiatrically ill father was found in the subgroup of unhappily married parents of mongols (Table 33). In no family where the marriage was rated as poor was more than one parent psychiatrically ill. The only family where both

Table 33

Parents' marital relationship and psychiatric illness

	Good	Moderate	Poor	TOTAL
A. Mothers of mongols				
Depressed	5	3	2	10
Not depressed	10	3	7	20
TOTAL	15	6	9	30
B. Fathers of mongols				
Psychiatrically ill	2	2	1	5
Well	13	4	8	25
TOTAL	15	6	9	30

X^2 tests = not significant

parents had depression during the two years after the birth of the mongol boy were in the most happily married group. This couple did not have symptoms at the same time and were able to help one another through the difficult periods.

Two men, who had both been hospitalized for psychiatric illnesses before the birth of the mongol, could well have been regarded as being especially at risk when confronted with the crisis presented by the birth of a child with a congenital abnormality. Both men did have a relapse but neither attributed the recurrence of symptoms to the stress of the birth of the child and both were happily married to warm and resilient women.

Although marital disharmony in the parents of these very young mongol children appears independent of formal psychiatric illnesses, unhappily married parents were likely to come into contact with doctors for a variety of complaints, which can be regarded as psychosomatic. Fathers were found to suffer from anxiety, depression and headaches whereas the mothers complained of migraine, weight loss, mennorrhagia, diarrhea and headaches, irritability and "nerves" and prolonged grief reaction. One father and two mothers were presented with clearly defined psychiatric problems.

Are the other children in the family affected by the parents' ill health or marital disharmony ?

The other children in the families into which a mongol baby was born were not found to have more behaviour or emotional problems than the children in the families with a normal baby. No effect can therefore be attributed to the presence of an abnormal baby, whether it is a direct or an indirect effect. Yet it might be expected that the children with problems would be more likely to come from homes with marital disharmony which has been shown to have a strong association with behaviour problems, particularly in boys (Rutter, 1970a).

How the teachers rated the siblings in both groups of families was not related to either the quality of the parents' marriage or to the presence of psychiatric illness in the parents. Of the five control children in the mongol group of siblings whose behaviour at school was rated as deviant, three were from families with a good marriage and one each from the moderate group of families and the families with poor marriages.

The parents' ratings of the siblings was strongly affected by the parents' own mental health, as shown by the incidence of psychiatric illness in parents but not by the quality of the parents' marital relationship (Table 34). There were five children in the mongol group with a parent with psychiatric illness and four of these had five or more symp-

Table 34

Parents' ratings of siblings' behavioural problems

| | Parent rating | | | |
| | Non-deviant | Deviant | | TOTAL |
	Score less than 5	Scores 5 to 9	10 +	
A. Parents' psychiatric illness				
Parental psychiatric illness	1	4	3	8
No parental psychiatric illness	26	7	1	34
TOTAL	27	11	4	42
$X^2 = 14 \cdot 13$, d.f. $= 2$, p $<0 \cdot 001$				
B. Parents' marital relationship				
Good	15	7	5	27
Moderate	7	3	1	11
Poor	1	3	0	4
TOTAL	23	13	6	42
$X^2 = 4 \cdot 423$, d.f. $= 4$, n.s.				

toms as rated by the parents. The three children in the control families with a psychiatrically ill parent all had five or more symptoms as rated by parents. A depressed mother, or one whose husband has a psychiatric illness, may be inclined to see more problems in the children, but on the other hand, the children could well be producing more symptoms of behavioural or emotional disturbance in reaction to the disturbance in the parents.

Factors Associated with the Baby or the Pregnancy and Subsequent Effects on the Parents

No factors in the baby itself such as the degree of hypotonia, the presence of congenital heart disease or management problems with feeding or behaviour were associated with parental psychiatric illness or marital disharmony in the families of the mongol children. Parents were also no more likely to be depressed or unhappily married if the mongol was the first born, if the mother was aged thirty-five or more at birth or if the pregnancy leading to the birth of the mongol was unplanned. Not at all surprising, however, is the finding that the birth of another baby in the follow-up period was more likely to have occurred in families where there was a warm and harmonious relationship between the parents.

How the Diagnosis Appeared to Affect Parenting Behaviour

No attempt was made to measure the degree of "acceptance" or "rejection" of the mongol babies. All the babies in this study received adequate physical care and all of them had at least one parent who showed clear evidence of warm parental feelings and nurturing behaviour. One father and one mother ceased to have any contact with the child but the other parent continued to care in each case. Another father would have nothing to do with his mongol son until the baby was six months old and then he became as devoted to the child as he was to the older boy. Two fathers had very little involvement in the case of the mongol boys and instead devoted themselves to the older children, thereby separating the two families into halves.

Several of the parents had a quite marked change of attitude and behaviour to the child as time elapsed and the child developed. One couple who had wanted to send back all the presents and cards they had received, so deeply diasppointed were they on hearing the news of the handicap, changed remarkably after the baby began to smile. Instead of wrapping her up so she could not be seen as they had previously, they dressed her prettily to introduce her to their neighbours, and the father laughingly admitted he came home half an hour earlier from work to enjoy the baby's playtime in her bath. Many fathers of normal babies are enchanted and deeply moved at the first "human response" of their baby but the fathers of the mongols had to wait much longer for that first smile.

During the first interviews, it was common to hear a mother or a father using generalizations about mongol children such as referring to "these children", "babies like her" or "others of his own kind". As time went on, these terms became less frequent. There were then many less comments about typical stigmata of Down's syndrome that the child may have had and more remarks alluding to the child's looks or habits that resembled those of other members of the family.

During the second year, two mothers, who had appeared to care most lovingly for the baby earlier on, said that they had taken a longer time to become as deeply attached to the mongol baby as they had to their other children. As one said "I did everything as it were mechanically" but then added "It is all right now as the right mother feelings came eventually as I went on looking after her." It is significant that it was only in the year after these attachment difficulties had resolved that the mothers were able to talk about such feelings.

A few parents had difficulty in naming the child once they knew that something serious was wrong. One family, as most families do, had a list of possible names drawn up in the pregnancy. The names were either those of close relatives or ones that were particularly attractive or meaningful to the parents. They had not quite made up their minds

which of these to give to the newborn child but when they were told of
the diagnosis of Down's syndrome, the list was abandoned. The child
had no name for nearly six weeks and then at the last minute before the
time of registration of the name was over, a "throw-away" name was
given that had a somewhat derogatory flavour to it.

Affectionate nicknames were common in the control families whose
normal babies would be addressed as "chubby-chops", "funny-face" or
by a reference to a well-known public figure. In contrast, the parents of
the mongol babies were very polite to their children. It was noticeable
that these loving insults were used by the nine parents when they had a
subsequent normal baby and a relaxation in their demeanour was very
obvious. One couple had noticed their baby's unusual appearance early
in life but had not realized the implication. They gave their son, who
was later diagnosed as a mongol, the nickname of "Chairman Mao".
They were both deeply distressed they had done this when it was pointed
out to them that the baby's appearance was characteristic of a patho-
logical condition. The parents both wept even a year later when they
were talking about this nickname.

The subsequent birth of a normal baby was the source of much satisfaction to the nine families in each group but to the parents in the
mongol group, the safe arrival of a perfectly formed child was an
immense relief after months of worry for all nine mothers, whether they
had had an amniocentesis or not. Only one of these mothers felt that the
birth of a new normal child had lessened her feeling for the handicapped
one. The others reported feeling much more relaxed, more able to wait
for the handicapped child to develop at his own pace and greatly reassured by their ability to produce a normal child.

In some cases, the behaviour of the mongol baby appeared to affect
parents differently than the same behaviour shown by a normal child.
The most striking example was the exploratory touching of the mother's
face with fingers poking into eyes and pulling hair. The normal children
all did this in the last quarter of the first year and the mothers, although
finding it uncomfortable, all saw it as learning the difference between
"self" which hurts if pinched and poked and "not self" which does not
hurt. Three mothers of mongols saw the same behaviour as definitely
aggressive and were afraid of what the child would do as he got older.

Five mothers were particularly concerned that the child should not
acquire the habit of protruding the tongue and spent time each day in
the latter part of the study fearfully watching for signs of this and "training" the child not to do it.

In general, the mothers and fathers of the mongol children were more
zealous about stimulating the baby. They provided mobiles for the chil-

dren to watch and other ingenious toys that rattled, squeaked or otherwise caught the child's attention. All but two felt their efforts to be rewarded. The two, already alluded to in this chapter, were both mothers of boys with severe hypotonia, major difficulties in feeding, very late in sitting (eighteen months and thirty months), and very slow to respond. The mothers of these two were older women, both over forty, with no supportive family behind them and with marriages, greatly lacking in warmth, to men who took no part in caring for the mongol child and had divided the family up by assuming the major role in caring for the normal children.

In general, the mongol baby as he grew up was treated as an ordinary member of the family, joining in all activities and being expected to learn to fit in with the others. One small mongol girl, the child of an enthusiastic pair of birdwatchers, was taken in a carrying pack on her father's back on regular weekend outings to the countryside as well as camping in a tent at holiday time. These ventures were considered a success until towards the end of the study some doubt was expressed by the parents concerning the effect of the child's chatter on the birds. In the first two years, the fact that the baby was abnormal was not reflected in any difference in the family outings or holidays enjoyed by the two groups of families.

Most mothers expressed a wish to train the handicapped child to behave socially as well as any other child. By the end of the study it was found that the mongol children did not disrupt other children's play any more than did the normal control children, and only eight of the mongols were considered destructive compared to fifteen of the normal children. No mother of a mongol at this stage found it necessary, or considered it right, to care for the handicapped child at the expense of others. Both the mothers, in the divided families where the father had assumed responsibility for the normal children, regretted the loss of close contact with the older ones.

In some areas it was the practice for young handicapped children to attend a special nursery class for a full day every day of the week from the age of two. One mother missed her baby when he started to go to the special nursery and kept her older normal boy back from his play group to have as a companion.

As they grew older, the small mongols were no more indulged than were the normal control children who were also the youngest in the family. Only in one family was there a different set of rules for the normal child and the mongol and the preferential treatment was definitely in favour of the normal child.

Some of the effects on parents and the rest of the family of the birth of an abnormal child can be qualified and shown to relate, or not to relate, to other effects or factors within the family. There are many other effects, particularly the more subtle ones on parents' attitudes and behaviour, that have so far defied attempts at any sort of objective measurement. Nonetheless these effects, as described in the latter part of this chapter, are interesting despite being somewhat nebulous. Only recently have there been well designed studies of human maternal behaviour with normal infants (Ciba Foundation Symposium 1974) and rarer still are studies of father's reactions to infants. The modification of the normal pattern of parenting behaviour by abnormality in the child awaits to be studied.

11 Conclusions and Recommendations

During the two year period between 1st January 1970 and 31st December 1971, thirty-one out of the forty babies known to have Down's syndrome and born in one administration area were taken home to be brought up within the family. The study involved following those families for the ensuing two years by a series of interviews carried out in the home. One family withdrew at the start of the study and three others were enrolled towards the end of the period and were only studied for eighteen months. The findings are compared with those from an individually matched group of families with normal babies.

The interviews included sections of a Family Investigation Interview which has been used in the study of children in the Isle of Wight, Camberwell and in other research projects (Brown and Rutter, 1966; Rutter *et al.*, 1970; Quinton *et al.*, 1976).

In addition other standardized questionnaires were used as well as rating scales developed for this particular study. The emphasis throughout was on fostering friendly relationships with the families, and particularly with the mother, to elicit information that could be recorded on tape. At first some of the parents were noticeably anxious and inclined to be on the defensive. As the interviews progressed, there was a gradual relaxation and willingness to discuss less comfortable topics. A very similar degree of rapport was established with the thirty control families with normal babies. Both groups were most co-operative and very generous with their time.

Baseline data about the functioning of a family before such an event as the birth of an abnormal child are inevitably retrospective and therefore liable to bias. To keep this bias to a minimum, questions about social activities and family interactions were strictly factual and applied only to the year immediately preceding the birth. Previous medical histories involved counts of actual admissions to hospital throughout life and visits to the general practitioner in the preceding year. No question was asked that implied any comparison between life as it was now with a mongol baby and life as it had been before the birth. There is no evidence from these baseline data collected in this way to suggest that the families into which a mongol baby was to be born had more psychiatric or physical morbidity or were more liable to family or general social dysfunction than were the control families who were to have normal babies.

Without exception, the parents experienced grief and shock when they first realized that their baby had a serious congenital abnormality and, in all probability, would grow up to be mentally retarded. Drotar *et al.* (1975) proposed a hypothetical model as a theoretical background for parental reactions to a congenitally malformed child with five stages —shock, denial, sadness and anger, adaptation, and reorganization. Similarly in this study the parents varied in the length of time required to pass through each stage to the next. A previous history of a psychiatric breakdown did not appear to influence the rate at which a parent achieved the final stage of reorganization, or positive acceptance, since the two men who had had previous admissions to a psychiatric hospital and who also had recurrences of their symptoms during the follow-up period were amongst the first to reach that stage.

The most striking, and most ominous, finding that emerged from the prospective study in this book is that the marriages of the couples who had a mongol baby were significantly more likely to be unhappy one year after the birth. As has been pointed out in Chapter 6, the number of marriages which were rated as good from the interview using the Brown and Rutter marital assessment, were similar in the two groups. The couples who did have a strong bond described themselves as drawn together by their shared sorrow at their child's abnormality, but the relationship between half the couples in the central group was also said to have deepened because of their mutual joy in a healthy baby. Harmonious marriages grew in strength through shared experience of both grief and happiness. The differences between the two groups lay in those rated "moderate" and those with overt disruption and hostility. The presence of a healthy baby appeared to keep the relationship jogging along with strains and tensions but no threat of breakdown. The abnormal child's birth, on the other hand, appeared to magnify pre-existing weaknesses thus turning stresses into obvious rifts. This adverse change in the relationship between the parents arose too soon to be directly concerned with the practical burden of caring for a handicapped child and appears more closely associated with the initial shock of the discovery of the abnormality. The five stage model put forward by Drotar *et al.* (1975) can assist in the understanding of the deterioration in the marriage relationships. One partner in five of the most unhappy marriages was still preoccupied with anger, usually projected against the medical profession, one year after the birth. Three other parents who had run away from the problem, two permanently and one temporarily, can be seen having trouble traversing a still earlier stage in the adjustment.

Morbidity in the parents of mongol babies was not found to be significantly higher than in parents of normal babies. The numbers in this study are small, but even including those women who were depressed but did not go to a doctor, the psychiatric morbidity of mothers of mongol children in the first two years of life does not exceed that found in mothers bringing up normal children in difficult circumstances. As the children get older and their development or behaviour markedly diverges from that of normal children, the strain on parents may produce more physical ill-health. Similarly, the small child with Down's syndrome does not present more difficulties for its siblings than does a normal child. Both normal and abnormal babies took up much of their mothers' time and, by the end of the period of study, five babies in each group were said to disturb the other children's play but nearly twice, fifteen, of the normal children were described as destructive at the age of two than were the mongols. The study of school age siblings of mongol children (Gath, 1973, 1974) indicated that older sisters were the most vulnerable and increased domestic burden was thought to be a possible factor in causing the disturbance in the girls. No evidence for higher parental expectations has been found for either girls or boys in the families in this study and it will be necessary to continue the follow-up to determine if more will be demanded of the normal sisters if and when the care of the handicapped child becomes much more arduous than that of a healthy child of the same age.

The future well-being of the siblings will be influenced by the parents' marital relationship. At this early stage disturbed siblings were not found to be more common where there was serious disharmony in the home, but other studies (Rutter, 1970a; Davie et al., 1972) have shown parental discord to have a close association with antisocial behaviour, particularly in boys. Two marriages broke down irretrievably during the first years after the birth of the affected baby but the future of the other unhappy marriages is uncertain. They may be going through a temporary deterioration from which they will recover to a state of relative stability, or the hostility and tension may persist and will eventually have adverse effects on the other children.

Less broken homes than expected were found among families of older children with Down's syndrome but this finding was balanced by the

excess number of divorces or separations in the families of similar children who had been admitted to the long stay mental subnormality hospitals in the same region. Although most long stay institutions have waiting
lists, evidence of "family stress" as shown in divorce or serious disharmony will favour the admission of a retarded child to hospital. The
problems in the home will also increase the chances of eventual institutionalization if the retarded child develops a reactive behaviour disorder.

In summary, it can be concluded that the birth of an abnormal child
does indeed bring shock and grief to parents and that this experience can
either bring them closer together or prove destructive to a more fragile
relationship. During the first two years of the infant's life there was no
significant excess of psychiatric or physical ill-health in parents or siblings in the families with a mongol child as compared with other families
of similar socio-economic status and size with a healthy baby of the same
age. There is therefore no evidence to suggest that the care in the home
of the infant with a congenital malformation such as Down's syndrome
will be at the expense of the health of either the parents or the normal
brothers and sisters. In addition, a small mongol child was not found to
be any greater restriction on the social activities of families than was a
normal baby.

In the past two years, published work reporting the stress on the
family of a handicapped child has led to some insensitive and unwarran-
ted assumptions that all families with such a child are in need of the
assistance of a social worker. Carr (1975) has drawn attention to the
impertinence of those who insist on offering therapy when what they are
asked for is factual information. Despite the understandable emotional
reaction to the fact of the baby's abnormality, most of the families in
this study have adjusted well and two years later are providing a home
environment that is stable and enriching for both their normal and
handicapped children. The findings of this study should not be interpreted as meaning that all parents with a child with a congenital malformation need either a marriage guidance counsellor or a psychiatrist.

A child with a congenital abnormality particularly associated with
mental retardation will become the concern during childhood of many
professional workers, including educators, psychologists, nurses, social
workers, psychiatrists and other medical specialists. No one profession
holds the key to their problems and a multi-disciplinary team approach
is essential for care of the best quality. The paediatrician, however, is in
a unique position at the most important time as it is most often he who
has to tell the parents of the diagnosis. The way this is done is important
and has been discussed in Chapter 4, where it is emphasized that making
a diagnosis should be the beginning of a programme of care, and not a

final, or once only, statement of bold facts. The management by paediatricians of babies with congenital malformations is currently being studied by Kennell (1976).

Unlike spina bifida or cleft lip and cleft palate, doctors have no cure or treatment for children with Down's syndrome, except those with the added problem of congenital heart disease. Parents in this study noticed the concentration of the doctors on this particular aspect of the syndrome and were often critical as it was not the most important issue to them.

There is therefore a problem with the parents wanting something done and the doctors feeling that they have little to offer. The children are too young for school or even pre-school or nursery care. Special education, involving psychologists and teachers, appears too far in the future. This hiatus in the care of the child between the medical treatment of an abnormal baby and the specialized education of a handicapped child can be discouraging to parents, who watch and wait for developmental milestones to be achieved so that they will know if the child is only mildly retarded or more severely affected. There have been some recent attempts to fill this gap. In England, Brinkworth has designed a programme to stimulate development (Brinkworth and Collins, 1969) and has produced a book to aid parents. In several centres in the United States, particularly in Seattle and Minneapolis, infant treatment placing much emphasis on parental involvement have been established. The parents whose children are attending such centres appear confident, optimistic and capable of deriving much satisfaction from caring for the handicapped children, but as far as is known there have been no controlled studies of the effects of such treatment centres on the mongol children or their families.

Special education on both sides of the Atlantic has grown particularly fast in the past ten years. Suitable educational placements are commonly available for most children within reasonable distance of their homes. Yet the parent of a new-born child with Down's syndrome rarely has had the opportunity of learning about these facilities and may still believe that the only future for their child is that of a hopeless life in an institution. The parents have to learn a great deal very fast and they have difficulty finding out how and where to obtain the information. It can happen that their advisors are almost as ignorant. Some paediatricians know little about special education and the general practitioner or health visitor may have only had one or two similar cases in their practices. The search for information led one father in this study to a public library shelf full of out of date medical textbooks which depressed him further and another father's fact collecting activities caused him to be labelled as "a disturbed and non-accepting parent". Acceptable books to give to parents are difficult to find but some are available providing facts and practical suggestions (see the list of recommended books at the end of this chapter).

The immediate needs of the parents of a child with a serious abnormality are first to be treated with honesty accompanied by compassion uncontaminated with condescension. They then require factual information so that they can make informed decisions and constructive support to allow them to use their own ways of coping with the problem. The support and the information may be needed over a period of time. A health visitor, whose special responsibility is the care of babies and their mothers, is an obvious source of support and should be able to offer some guidance, but she too will need to be able to refer elsewhere for further help. The ordinary paediatric out-patient clinic has not been seen as very helpful by the parents in this study. An alternative is the developmental clinic where children with a variety of developmental problems can be seen with their parents by specialists from different disciplines. Such clinics have been designed with good waiting areas and playrooms for observation and may be the place where such facilities as toy libraries can be found. If these centres can also be used for the professionals involved as training centres, and as places where parents can be involved in treatment, much could be achieved without excessive expenditure. In more rural areas similar combined clinics can utilize local health centres which have advantages of being proximal, familiar and less threatening than larger specialist centres. The number of clinic attendances could be kept to a minimum if the original evaluation involved the health visitor making her an essential part of the care plan and providing her with a base to which she can refer, and from which she can learn. The paediatrician is usually at the centre of such a developmental clinic and will involve other specialists in paediatric cardiology, ophthalmology, orthopaedics and clinical psychology as necessary. In this study one general practitioner provided his own clinical service for the Down's children in his practice, and he referred elsewhere when the need for a specialized evaluation arose.

There is still unfortunately a gap between the management of the physical anomalies and the evaluation and treatment of the mental retardation, which most parents understandably regard as the major problem. The specialists in mental handicap had very little part to play in this study of thirty families and the only intervention was not very successful. By the end of the two years, most parents were still fearful about institutionalization and regarded referral to the mental handicap specialist as a threat. Child psychiatrists, including those with interests in children of all mental abilities, are, with a few notable exceptions, only beginning to work constructively in partnership with their paediatric colleagues. There are, however, encouraging signs in Britain and in the United States of a new interest in links between the specialists caring for the minds and bodies of children.

It is not the psychiatrists or even psychologists who are the main participants in the treatment of mental retardation but teachers. No treatment programme for children with mental retardation and their families can be planned without being based on a sound educational plan.

One crucial question remains unanswered. How can the families who will be torn apart by the advent of a handicapped child be first detected and then helped? In many ways the families who are particularly vulnerable in this situation are also those who are liable to break down in adverse circumstances. In discussing early detection of the potential child abuser, Steele (1974) suggested that those caring for pregnant women should look out for those who were socially isolated, had had little experience of being warmly mothered themselves and had a joyless relationship with their husband. Although it was detachment rather than attacks of rage towards the child that worried some mothers, the screening criteria above fits the most unhappy mothers. The information can be elicited in a way that is gentle, non-intrusive and yet reliable (MacFarlane, 1977).

A second method of detection uses the finding that vague psychiatric symptoms, and particularly psychosomatic symptoms, are associated with the very poor marital ratings as seen in Chapter 6. Family doctors who know about the health of the whole family, as well as the problems of the affected child, should be aware of the problems behind the symptoms. Some doctors are glad to do some marital counselling themselves, but others will prefer to ask the advice of marriage guidance counsellors or a psychiatrist with a special interest in marital therapy.

It has been suggested before, and can be stressed again, that straightforward handling of parents with trust and respect on both sides does much to dispel confusion and hopelessness. Perhaps the best way to help the parents is not by minimizing or avoiding the problems, but to give them direction and something to do. Important contributions are provided by infant stimulation programmes, handicapped children's classes, day centres and home visiting schemes. Most families will cope with such circumstances and should not be treated as potential psychiatric patients or social work clients. Therapy should be reserved for the more vulnerable parents who can be identified by a sensitive observer. For them the birth represents a major crisis in their lives and may reopen many old wounds. At this time both parents are in need of therapeutic help which may prove particularly beneficial.

A crisis can be considered as a transitional period (Brandon, 1970) in which an individual can either make significant gains in personality growth or may suffer adversely with increased vulnerability to stress in the future. The theory behind psychiatric intervention at the time of crisis has been developed by Caplan 1961, 1964a,b. When the equilibrium of a person's life is threatened, the initial reaction is to utilize customary methods to cope with the threat. A crisis develops when these everyday methods fail. The first stage of the crisis consists of increasing tension accompanied by feelings of discomfort. As the tension increases in the second stage, some disorganization occurs. There is loss of effectiveness and the appearance of subjective experiences of anxiety, fear, shame or guilt. More activity develops in the third stage when emergency problem solving techniques are called up, the problem is looked at again from different directions and much effort is put into finding a solution. Once found, the solution may not be ideal and may be either incomplete or inappropriate. Under normal circumstances some sort of resolution occurs within a certain time limit, usually of four to six weeks. If no solution is found, more serious disorganization or "breakdown" will occur, which is Caplan's fourth theoretical stage. This theory has been discussed in relation to a variety of stresses. Crisis theory depends in part upon theories of personality development, particularly that of Erikson (1965) in which the child copes with inevitable crises at various developmental stages. Studies of grief (Lindemann, 1944; Murray Parkes, 1964) also contribute in an important way. The implication for treatment ties in the hypothesis that the person undergoing the crisis is particularly susceptible to change during the second stage of initial disorganization, increased dependency and lack of effectiveness. Not only is therapy at this time more effective than in more quiet phases of life but it is also more acceptable.

Drotar *et al.* (1975) suggest that the first days after learning of the child's handicap constitute just such a crisis and that help given at the time will prevent further disintegration and may well lead to positive gain. Although as we have seen most parents cope very adequately with this stress, provided that they are dealt with in an open and positive way, for the vulnerable minority, however, it is a "make or break" situation with all the theoretical characteristics of a crisis. Skilled intervention must quickly follow prompt recognition of those in trouble. Most maternity units now have social workers attached. They need to work closely with the paediatrician, to be present or very near at hand when the parents are told of the diagnosis, so that they can detect signs of disorganization and recognize the more vulnerable or precarious relationships. Close liaison with psychiatric services should then ensure that effective therapy for the crisis situation takes place when the need arises.

The impetus for much of the improvement in services for mentally handicapped children over recent years has come from parents who have been able to exert considerable influence on the professionals. The emphasis on the care of the mentally handicapped child has changed from the medically dominated, institutional approach to one in which the axiom is "These children are children first and mentally handicapped second" (National Development Group for the MentallyHandicapped, 1977). The baby with Down's syndrome appears to challenge the family to accept it as first and foremost a baby with full family membership. Most families can cope with this challenge provided that they are shown a path ahead for themselves and their child. The few who will have difficulty coping can be identified and offered appropriate help.

Books for Parents

Brinkworth, R. and Collins, J. E. (1969). "Improving Mongol Babies and Introducing them to School." National Society for Mentally Handicapped Children, Belfast.

Horrobin, J. M. and Rynders, J. E. (1974). "To Give an Edge. A Guide for New Parents of Down's Syndrome (Mongoloid) Children." Colwel Press, Inc., Minneapolis.

Jeffree, D. and McConkey, R. (1976). "Let Me Speak." Souvenir Press, London.

Solly, K. (1972). "The Different Baby." Millbrook Press.

References

Alberman, E. (1975). The prevention of Down's syndrome. *Dev. Med. Child Neurol.* **17**, 793–795.

Aldrich, C. A. (1947). Preventive medicine and mongolism. *Am. J. Ment. Defic.* **52**, 127–129.

Antley, R. M. and Hartlage, L. C. (1976). Psychological responses to genetic counselling for Down's syndrome. *Clin. Genet.* **9**, 257–265.

Ashley Miller, J. (1971). Coming through a crisis. *The Times.* October 11th.

Barsch, R. H. (1968). "The Parent of the Handicapped Child." Charles C. Thomas, Springfield, Illinois.

Berg, J. M. and Kirman, B. H. (1961). Risk of dual occurrence of mongolism in sibships. *Arch. Dis. Child.* **36**, 645.

Berg, J. M., Gilderdale, S. and Way, J. (1969). On telling parents of a diagnosis of mongolism. *Br. J. Psychiatr.* **115**, 1195–1196.

Bobrow, M. (1977). Genetic counselling: a tool for the prevention of some abnormal pregnancies. *J. Clin. Pathol.* **29** (Suppl. 10), 145–149.

Bowlby, J. (1951). "Child Care and the Growth of Love." Penguin, London.

Brandon, S. (1970). Crisis theory and possibilities of therapeutic intervention. *Br. J. Psychiatr.* **117**, 627–633.

Brinkworth, R. and Collins, J. E. (1969). "Improving Mongol Babies and Introducing them to School." Nat. Soc. Ment. Handicapped Child., Belfast.

Brown, G. W. and Rutter, M. (1966). The measurement of family activities and relationships—a methodological study. *Hum. Relat.* **19**, 241–263.

Buck, P. S. (1951). "The Child who Never Grew." Methuen, London.

Burton, L. (1975). "The Family Life of Sick Children." Routledge and Kegan Paul, London.

Butler, N. R. and Alberman, E. D. (1969). "Perinatal Problems." Livingstone, London.

Caldwell, B. M. and Guze, S. B. (1960). A study of the adjustment of parents and siblings of institutionalized and non-institutionalized retarded children. *Am. J. Ment. Defic.* **64**, 845–861.

Caplan, G. (Ed.) (1961). "Prevention of Mental Disorders in Children." Basic Books, New York.

Caplan, G. (1964a). "An Approach to Community Mental Health." Tavistock Publications, London.

Caplan, G. (1964b). "Principles of Preventive Psychiatry." Tavistock Publications, London.

Carey, W. B. (1970). A simplified method for measuring infant temperament. *Pediatrics* **77**, 188–194.

Carr, J. (1970). Mongolism: telling the parents. *Dev. Med. Child Neurol.* **12**, 213.

Carr, J. (1975). "Young Children with Down's Syndrome." Butterworth's, London.

Cartwright, A. (1970). "Parents and Family Planning Services." Routledge and Kegan Paul, London.

Centerwall, S. A. and Centerwall, W. R. (1960). A study of children with mongolism reared in the home compared with those reared away from the home. *Pediatrics* **25**, 678–685.

Clarke, A. M. and Clarke, A. D. B. (1974). "Mental Deficiency: The Changing Outlook." Methuen, London.

Clarke, C. M., Edwards, J. H. and Smallpiece, V. (1961). 21 Trisomy/normal mosaicism in an intelligent child with mongoloid characters. *Lancet* **1** (7185), 1028.

Collman, R. D. and Stoller, A. (1962). A survey of mongoloid births in Victoria, Australia 1942–57. *Am. J. Publ. Health.* **52,** 813.

Cowie, V. A. (1970). "A Study of the Early Development of Mongols." Inst. Res. Ment. Retard., Monogr. No. 1. Pergamon, London.

Cox, A., Rutter, M., Newman, S. and Bartak, L. (1975). A comparative study of infantile autistic and specific developmental receptive language disorders. II. Parental charactersitics. *Br. J. Psychiatr.* **126,** 146–159.

Cummings, S. T., Bayley, H. C. and Rie, H. E. (1966). Effects of the child's deficiency on the mother: a study of mothers of mentally retarded, chronically ill and neurotic children. *Am. J. Orthopsych.* **36,** 595–608.

D'Arcy, E. (1968). Congenital defects: mothers' reactions to first information. *Br. Med. J.* **3,** 796–798.

Davie, R., Butler, N. and Goldstein, H. (1972). "From Birth to Seven." Longman, London.

Davies, P. A., Robinson, R. J., Scopes, J. W., Tizard, J. P. M. and Wigglesworth, J. S. (1972). "Medical Care of Newborn Babies." Spastics International Medical Publications. Heinemann, London.

Davis, F. (1963). "Passage Through Crisis." The Bobbs-Merrill Company, Inc., Indianapolis.

de Lange, S. A. (1975). The management of spina bifida aperta. *Oxford Med. Sch. Gaz.* **27,** 75–76.

Dominian, J. (1968). "Marital Breakdown." Penguin, London.

Drillien, C. M. and Wilkinson, E. N. (1964a). Emotional stress and mongoloid births. *Dev. Med. Child. Neurol.* **6,** 140–143.

Drillien, C. M. and Wilkinson, E. N. (1964b). Mongolism: when should parents be told? *Br. Med. J.* **2,** 1306.

Drotar, D., Baskiewicz, A., Irvin, N., Kennell, J. and Klaus, M. (1975). The adaptation of parents to the birth of an infant with a congenital malformation: a hypothetical model. *Pediatrics* **56,** 710–717.

Erikson, E. H. (1965). "Childhood and Society." Penguin, London.

Erikson, M. T. (1969). M.M.P.I. profiles of parents of young retarded children. *Am. J. Ment. Defic.* **73,** 728–732.

Farber, B. (1959). The effects of a severely mentally retarded child on family integration. *Mon. Soc. Res. Child Dev.* **24** (2).

Farber, B. and Jenne, W. C. (1963). Family organisation and parent–child communication: parents and siblings of a retarded child. *Mon. Soc. Res. Child Dev.* **28** (7).

Farber, B. and Rykman, D. R. (1965). Effects of severely mentally retarded children on family relationships. *Ment. Retard. Abst.* **2,** 1–17.

Farrell, M. (1956). The adverse effects of early institutionalization of mentally subnormal children. *Am. J. Dis. Child.* **91,** 278–281.

Fletcher, R. (1975). Moral and ethical problems of prenatal diagnosis. *Clin. Genet.* **8,** 251–257.

Fletcher, R. (1962). "The Family and Marriage in Britain." Penguin, London.

Ford, E. H. R. (1972). "Human Chromosomes." Academic Press, London and New York.

Fowle, C. M. (1969). The effect of the severely retarded child on his family. *Am. J Ment. Defic.* **73,** 468.

Franklin, A. W. (1963). Physically handicapped babies. Some thalidomide lessons. *Lancet* **1** (7288), 959–962.

Fraser, F. C. and Latour, A. (1968). Birth rates in families following the birth of a child with mongolism. *Am. J. Ment. Defic.* **72,** 883–886.

Freeston, B. M. (1971). An enquiry into the effect of a spina bifida child upon family life. *Dev. Med. Child Neurol.* **13,** 456.

Frommer, E. A. and O'Shea, G. (1973). Antenatal identification on women liable to have problems in managing their infants. *Br. J. Psychiatr.* **123,** 149–156.

Gath, A. (1972a). The effects of mental subnormality on the family. *In* "Contemporary Psychiatry" (Eds Silverstone, T. and Barraclough, B.). Headley Brothers, London.

Gath, A. (1972b). The mental health of siblings of a congenitally abnormal child. *J. Child Psychol. Psychiatr.* **13,** 211–218.

Gath, A. (1973). The schoolage siblings of mongol children. *Br. J. Psychiatr.* **123,** 161–167.

Gath, A. (1974). Sibling reactions to mental handicap: a comparison of the brothers and sisters of mongol children. *J. Child Psychol. Psychiatr.* **15,** 187–198.

Goldberg, D. P. (1972). "The Detection of Psychiatric Illness by Questionnaire." Maudsley Monogr. 21, Oxford University Press.

Goldie, L. (1966). The psychiatry of the handicapped family. *Dev. Med. Child Neurol.* **8,** 456.

Goldfarb, W. (1945). Effects of psychological deprivation in infancy and subsequent stimulation. *Am. J. Psychiatr.* **102,** 18–33.

Graliker, B. V., Fishler, K. and Koch, R. (1962). Teenage reaction to a mentally retarded sibling. *Am. J. Ment. Defic.* **66,** 838–843.

Green, M. (1966). "Elizabeth." Hodder and Stoughton, London.

Hannam, C. (1975). "Parents and Mentally Handicapped Children." Penguin, London.

Harlow, H. F. and Harlow, M. K. (1969). Effects of various mother–infant relationships on Rhesus monkey behaviours. *In* "Determinants of Infant Behaviour" (Ed. B. M. Foss), Vol. 4. Methuen, London.

Hewett, S. (1970). "The Family and the Handicapped Child." Allen and Unwin, London.

Holt, K. S. (1957). The impact of mentally retarded children on their families. M.D. Thesis, University of Manchester.

Hunt, N. (1967). "The World of Nigel Hunt." Darwen-Finlayson, Chichester.

Jenkins, R. (1933). Etiology of mongolism. *Am. J. Dis. Child.* **45,** 506.

Kanner, L. (1953). Parents' feelings about retarded children. *Am. J. Ment. Defic.* **57,** 375–383.

Kaplan, F. (1969). Siblings of the retarded. *In* "Psychological Problems in Mental Deficiency" (Ed. S. B. Sarason). Harper and Row, New York.

Kempe, C. H. and Helfer, R. E. (Eds) (1972). "Helping the Battered Child and his Family." Lippincott, Philadelphia.

Kennell, J. and Klaus, M. (1974). Care of the mother of the high risk infant. *Clin. Obst. Gynaecol.* **14,** 926–954.

Kennell, J. (1976). Personal communication.

Korner, A. F. (1973). Sex differences in new borns with special reference to differences in the organisation of oral behaviour. *J. Child Psychol. Psychiatr.* **14,** 19–29.

Kramm, E. (1963). "Families of Mongoloid Children." Child. Bur., U.S. Dep. Health, Ed. and Welfare, Washington, D.C.

Krovetz, L. J., Gessner, I. H. and Schiebler, G. L. (1969). "Pediatric Cardiology" Harper and Row, New York.

Lejeune, J., Gautier, M. and Turpin, R. (1959). Etudes des chromosomes somatiques de neuf enfants mongoliens. C.R. Acad. Sci. 248, 1721.

Leonard, C. O., Chase, G.A. and Childs, B. (1972). Genetic counselling: a consumer's view. New England J. Med. 287, 433–439.

Leiderman, P. H. (1974). Mothers at risk: a potential consequence of the hospital care of the premature infant. In "The Child in his Family: Children at Psychiatric risk" (Eds. Anthony E. J. and Koupernik, C.). John Wiley, London.

Lilienfield, A. M. (1969). "Epidemiology of Mongolism." John Hopkins Press, Baltimore.

Lindemann, E. (1944). Symptomatology and management of acute grief. Am. J. Psychiatr. 101, 141.

Lorber, J. (1971). Results of treatment of myelomeningocele. An analysis of 524 unselected cases, with special reference to possible selection for treatment. Dev. Med. Child Neurol. 13, 279.

Lindenbaum, R. (1977). Personal communication.

Lyle, J. G. (1959). The effects of an institution upon the verbal development of imbecile children. I. Verbal intelligence. J. Ment. Defic. Res. 3, 122–128.

Lyle, J. G. (1960a). The effects of an institution upon the verbal development of imbecile children. II. Speech and Language. J. Ment. Defic. Res. 4, 1–13.

Lyle, J. G. (1960b). The effects of an institution upon the verbal development of imbecile children. III. The Brooklands Residential family unit. J. Ment. Defic. Res. 4, 14–23.

MacFarlane, J. A. (1977). "The Psychology of Childbirth." Fontana, London.

Matsunaga, E. (1967). Parental Age, Live-Birth Order and Pregnancy-Free Interval in Down's Syndrome in Japan. Mongolism. Ciba Foundation Study Group No. 25. J. and A. Churchill, London.

Minde, K. K., Hacket, J. D., Killou, D. and Silver, S. (1972). How they grow up: 41 physically handicapped children and their families. Am. J. Psychiatr. 128, 1554–1560.

Morris, P. (1969). "Put Away: A Sociological Study of Institutions for the Mentally Retarded." Routledge and Kegan Paul, London.

Murray Parkes, C. (1964). Effects of bereavement on physical and mental health—a study of the medical records of widows. Br. Med. J. 2, 274–279.

National Association for Mental Health Working Party (1971). The birth of an abnormal child: telling the parents. Lancet 2 (7733), 1075–1077.

National Development Group for the Mentally Handicapped (1977)." Mentally Handicapped Children: A Plan for Action." Pamphlet No. 2.

Osmin, M. (1971). "The Empty Hours: A Study of the Weekend Life of Handicapped Children in Institutions." Penguin, London.

Owens, D., Dowson, J. C. and Losin, S. (1971). Alzheimer's Disease in Down's Syndrome. Am. J. Ment. Defic. 75, 606.

Penrose, L. S. (1933). The relative effects of paternal and maternal age in mongolism. J. Genet. 27, 219.

Penrose, L. S. (1938). "A Clinical and Genetic Study of 1280 Cases of Mental Defect." Spec. Rep. Ser. Med. Res. Coun. No. 229. H.M.S.O., London.

Penrose, L. S. (1961). Mongolism. Br. Med. Bull. 17, 184.

Penrose, L. S. (1967). Studies of mosaicism in Down's anomaly. *In* "Mental Retardation" (Ed. G. A. Jewis). Charles C. Thomas, Springfield.

Penrose, L. S. (1969). "Biology of Mental Defect" (Revised edn). Sidgewick and Jackson, London.

Penrose, L. S. (1970). Personal communication.

Penrose, L. S. (1972). Personal communication.

Penrose, L. S. and Smith, G. F. (1966). "Down's Anomaly." Churchill, London.

Polani, P. E., Briggs, J. H., Clarke, C. M. and Berg, J. M. (1960). A mongol girl with 46 chromosomes. *Lancet* **1**, (7127), 721.

Quinton, D., Rutter, M. and Rowlands, O. (1976). An evaluation of an interview assessment of marriage. *Psychol. Med.* **6**, 577–586.

Richman, N. and Graham, P. J. (1971). A behavioural screening questionnaire for use with three year old children. Preliminary findings. *J. Child Psychol. Psychiatr.* **12**, 5–33.

Rutter, M. (1967). A children's behaviour questionnaire for completion by teachers: preliminary findings. *J. Child. Psychol. Psychiatr.* **8**, 1–11.

Rutter, M. (1970a). Sex differences in children's responses to family stress. *In* "The Child and His Family" (Eds E. J. Anthony, C. Koupernik). International Year Book for Child Psychiatry, London.

Rutter, M. (1970b). Family size, structure and composition as factors in deviant child development. Internat. Assoc. Child Psychol. and Psychiatr., Jerusalem.

Rutter, M. and Brown, G. W. (1966). The reliability and validity of measures of family life and relationships in families containing a psychiatric patient. *Soc. Psychiatr.* **1**, 38–53.

Rutter, M., Tizard, J. and Whitmore, K. (1970). "Education, Health and Behaviour." Longman, London.

Rutter, M., Cox, A., Tupling, C., Berger, M. and Yale, W. (1975). Attainment and adjustment in two geographical areas. I. The prevalence of psychiatric disorder. *Br. J. Psychiatr.* **126**, 493–509.

Sameroff, A. and Chandler, H. J. (1974). Reproduction risk and the continuum of child caring casualty. *In* "Review of Child Development" (Eds F. D. Horowitz, M. Hetherington, S. Scan-Salapalek and G. Siegel), Vol. 4. University of Chicago.

Schonell, F. J. and Watts, B. H. (1957). A first survey on the effects of a subnormal child on the family unit. *Am. J. Ment. Defic.* **61**, 210–219.

Scully, C. (1973). Down's Syndrome. *Br. J. Hosp. Med.* **10**, 89.

Seguin, E. (1866). Quoted by Penrose (1969).

Shipe, D. and Shotwell, A. M. (1964). Effect of out-of-home care on the intellectual and social development of mongoloid children. *Am. J. Ment. Defic.* **68**, 693.

Shuttleworth, G. E. (1909). Mongolian imbecility. *Br. Med. J.* **2**, 661.

Siegel, S. (1956). "Non Parametric Statistics for the Behavioural Sciences." McGraw-Hill, New York.

Skodak, M. and Skeels, H. M. (1949). A final follow up study of one hundred adopted children. *J. Genet. Psychol.* **75**, 85–125.

Slutsky, H. (1969). Maternal reaction and adjustment to birth and care of a cleft palate child. *Cleft Palate J.* **6**, 425–429.

Smith, A. and McKeown, T. (1955). Prenatal growth of mongoloid defectives. *Arch. Dis. Child.* **30**, 257–259.

Solnit, A. J. and Stark, M. H. (1961). Mourning and the birth of a defective child. *Psychoanalyt. Stud. Child* **16**, 523–537.

Stedman, D. J. and Eichorn, D. H. (1964). A comparison of the growth and development of institutionalised and home reared mongoloids during infancy and child-hood. *Am. J. Ment. Defic.* **69**, 391–401.

Steele, B. and Pollock, C. (1974). A psychiatric study of parents who abuse infants and small children. *In* "The Battered Child" (Eds R. E. Helfer, C. H. Kempe). University of Chicago Press.

Stein, Z., Susser, M. and Guterman, A. V. (1973). Screening programme for prevention of Down's syndrome. Lancet 1 (7798), 305.

Stone, D. H. (1972). The birth of a child with Down's syndrome: a medico-social pilot study of thirty one children and their families. *Br. Med. J.* prize for medical students essay.

Stott, D. H. (1957). Physical and mental handicap following a disturbed pregnancy. *Lancet* 1 (6977), 1006.

Stott, D. H. (1961). Mongolism related to emotional shock in early pregnancy. *Vita Hun.* **4**, 57.

Stott, D. H. (1973). Follow up study from birth of the effects of prenatal stress. *Dev. Med. Child Neurol.* **15**, 770–787.

Tew, B., Payne, E. H. and Lawrence, K. M. (1974). Must a family with a handicapped child be a handicapped family? *Dev. Med. Child Neurol.* **16** (Suppl. 32), 95–98.

Thomas, A., Chess, S. and Birch, H. G. (1968). "Temperament and Behaviour Disorders in Children." University of New York, Massachusetts.

Tizard, J. (1960). Residential care of mentally handicapped children. *Br. Med. J.* **1,** 1041.

Tizard, J. and Grad, J. C. (1961). "The Mentally Handicapped and their Families." Maudsley Mon. 7, London.

Turnbull, A. C. and Woodford, F. P. (1976). "Review of Research Practice" Vol. 18. Elsevier, Amsterdam.

Vesey, M. (1975). Personal communication.

Werner, E. E., Bierman, J. M. and French, F. E. (1971). "The Children of Kauai, Honolulu." University of Hawaii.

Wedge, P. and Prosser N. (1973). "Born to Fail?" Arrow Books, London.

Wilks, J. and Wilks, E. (1974). "Bernard. Bringing up our Mongol Son." Routledge and Kegan Paul, London.

Wolfensberger, W. (1968). "Counselling the Parents of the Retarded in Mental Retardation: Appraisal, Rehabilitation and Education" (Ed. A. A. Baumeister). University of London Press.

Younghusband, E., Birchall, D., Davie, R. and Kellmer Pringle, H. L. (1970). "Living with Handicap." National Bureau for Co-operation in Child Care.

Subject Index

SOCIAL SCIENCE LIBRARY

Manor Road Building
Manor Road
Oxford OX1 3UQ
Tel: (2)71093 (enquiries and renewals)
http://www.ssl.ox.ac.uk

This is a **NORMAL LOAN** item.

We will email you a reminder before this item is due.

Please see http://www.ssl.ox.ac.uk/lending.html
for details on:

- loan policies; these are also displayed on the notice boards and in our library guide.

- how to check when your books are due back.

- how to renew your books, including information on the maximum number of renewals.
Items may be renewed if not reserved by another reader. Items must be renewed before the library closes on the due date.

- level of fines; fines are charged on overdue books.

Please note that this item may be recalled during Term.